English   Furniture

E. T. Joy

English furniture

A.D. 43-1950

B. T. Batsford Ltd

LONDON

Matri meae

First published 1962
Reprinted 1987

PRINTED AND BOUND IN GREAT BRITAIN BY
R. J. ACFORD LTD, CHICHESTER, WEST SUSSEX
FOR THE PUBLISHERS
B. T. BATSFORD LTD,
4 FITZHARDINGE STREET, LONDON W1H 0AH

ISBN 0 7134 5842 9

Introduction

HORACE WALPOLE's description of the furniture in Hogarth's pictures as 'the history of the manners of the age' is equally valid for furniture at all times, for it is a subject which, as the visible embodiment of everyday life, makes an ideal introduction to social history. Even scarcity of furniture—and for most of their history most English people have had little enough—tells its story of the roughness and discomfort of life.

Furniture is also a barometer of taste; its changes of design and decoration reflect the influence of artistic movements, both foreign and English, the use, effective or otherwise, of many materials, and the varying standards of the craftsman's skill.

It is with reference to social conditions, the craftsmen, and the genesis and growth of styles, that this book attempts an introductory survey of the history of English furniture. It is hoped that it may be of use to students of social history and to all who are interested in furniture. Its introductory nature needs to be stressed, for there remains much work to do in connection with it —museums and houses to visit, pieces of furniture and decoration to look at, sketch and photograph, and books to consult for further study.

I should like to express my appreciation to Mr Michael Barnes for his meticulous care with the line drawings, to Mr E. F. Marshall, Principal of Shoreditch Training College, for opportunities readily offered and gratefully accepted, to Miss T. M. Nye, for seeing the book so admirably through the press, and to my wife for compiling the index.

London 1962   E. T. J.

Contents

Acknowledgment

The Author and Publishers wish to thank all those who have helped in any way in the preparation of this book, and the following who have given their permission for the artist to make sketches of various pieces of furniture or for particular photographs to be reproduced:

The Trustees of the Roman Museum (Bath) for figs 1, 3 and 4

Anthony Bird for figs **161** and **175**

Edward Barnsley for figs **193**, **194**, **195**, **196** and 199

H. Blairman & Sons Ltd for figs **119** and **132**

B. C. Clayton for figs **9, 10, 11** and **12**

The Trustees of the Geffrye Museum for fig. 42

Messrs Heal's of Tottenham Court Road, London, for fig. **197**

M. Harris & Sons for fig. **131**

The Directors of Pepys Library, Magdalene College, Cambridge, for fig. 74

Gordon Russell for fig. 198

The Trustees of the Victoria and Albert Museum (photographs Crown Copyright) for figs 6, 13, 16, 17, 21, 23, 33, 34, 36, 37, 38, 39, **46**, 47, 48, 49, 65, 66, 79, 81, 84, 101, 106, 107, 108, 110, 121, 122, 130, **147**, 157, **176**, 181, 184, **185**, **186**, **187**, **188**, 190, 191, 192

The Dean and Chapter of Westminster Abbey for fig. 7

Denys Wrey Limited for fig. **111**

The numerals in **bold** *refer to the photographs*

Some terms defined

Bolection moulding Raised moulding, usually of ogee shape (i.e. concave below, convex above) used above surface of framework enclosing panel.

Cabriole leg (Fr. 'goat's leap') Curved support with rounded knee and concave curve below, used on English furniture *c.* 1700–60.

Case furniture Fitted pieces, e.g. cabinets, chests of drawers, etc., as opposed to seat furniture, tables and beds.

Cavetto moulding Hollow moulding often found on cornice of case furniture in late seventeenth and eighteenth centuries.

Chinoiserie General term for European decorative work in the Chinese taste.

Finial Knob ornament, often vase-shaped, used on platform intersecting stretchers of chairs and tables in late seventeenth century, and on top of case furniture.

Gadrooning Repetitive ornamental edging of convex form used on sixteenth-century oak furniture (e.g. on bulbous supports and edges of court cupboards) and again in eighteenth century.

Gesso Composition of chalk and parchment size applied to furniture and carved and gilded, *c.* 1690–1725.

Japanning European imitation of oriental lacquer (q.v.)

Lacquer Oriental method of decorating furniture with gum-lac dissolved in spirits, producing glossy and highly coloured finish.

Lazy-tongs Zig-zag levers which can be folded and extended, used to extend tables in the Regency period.

Ormolu (Fr. 'ground gold') Brightly gilded bronze and brass mounts, first made in England by M. Boulton after 1760, extensively used in Adam and Hepplewhite periods.

Patera Classical round or oval disk ornament, applied, carved or painted, widely used in Adam period.

Splat Upright structural member in centre of chair-back.

Stretcher Horizontal bar joining and strengthening legs of tables and chairs.

The Furniture of Roman Britain

A.D. 43–c. 410

THE oldest surviving furniture of any kind in Britain is that of the Early Bronze Age (c. 1900–1700 B.C.), and consists of very simple stone pieces, including box-beds and dressers, which were uncovered in the village of Skara Brae in the Orkneys. It is possible that wooden furniture of a rudimentary kind may also have been made in prehistoric times with the various tools (first of stone, then of bronze and iron), which were in use, but any such pieces, if ever made, have long since perished. In fact, from the time of Skara Brae until well after the Norman Conquest there is, with the exception of the period of the Roman occupation, an almost complete dearth of evidence of furniture, with the practical conclusion that very little was used.

The four centuries of the Roman occupation of Britain gave much of the country the conditions which have encouraged the development of domestic furniture—stability, prosperity, urban life and a cultured upper class. After the collapse of Roman rule in the fifth century and the coming of the Anglo-Saxons these conditions were largely absent for nearly a thousand years. Certainly the standards of furnishing, interior decoration, sanitation and central heating found in the larger Romano-British town houses and in the villas (which were centres of country estates and linked

economically and socially with the towns as were, much later, the Palladian country houses of Georgian England) were not equalled until recent times. Thus Romano-British furniture is an interlude and a foretaste, but not a direct forerunner, of subsequent furniture.

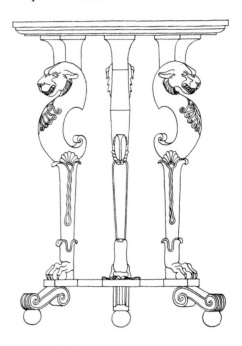

2 Classical table with animal monopodia
(from T. Hope 1807)

No complete pieces of furniture have survived from the Roman period, but fragments discovered by archaeologists, and the sculptured furniture on tombstones and statuary, make it clear that Roman Britain had the same kind of furniture which was in use throughout western Europe at the time, and which was itself largely inherited from the older civilisations of Egypt and Greece. From Egypt came the advanced technical skills of veneering, gilding, turning, the panel and frame construction and the mortise and tenon joint; from Greece, beauty of form and decoration.

The rare surviving fragments of actual furniture of Roman Britain include iron and bronze bands,

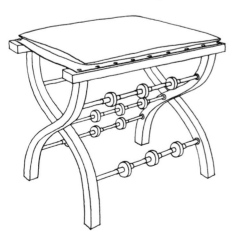

1 Roman folding stool made in wood or metal

I

3 Roman wicker chair

backs and sides, many of them made of wicker (3); straight-backed chairs; footstools; and small, three-legged tables (4). We can assume the existence of other wooden pieces long-vanished, such as various forms of chairs, stools, tables and cupboards. There was no lack of upholstery materials which, like the furniture, were both imported and home-made.

In the wealthier houses, in a setting of mosaic floors and of painted plaster or panelled walls, this furniture had a degree of elegance and craftsmanship which was not recaptured until the Georgian period. It has more than a passing academic interest, for its forms were revived in England at the time of Trafalgar and Waterloo, when in the archaeological phase of the Regency style designers copied actual pieces of classical furniture.

handles, hinges, locks and feet used on wooden chests and caskets; iron folding stools (1); stone supports for benches and tables; and legs and panels of Kimmeridge shale. These legs, of animal form with claw feet, resemble the outward-curved animal (2) and winged griffin monopodia on tables found at Herculaneum and Pompeii. Shale seems to have been a widely used furniture material which could be turned and carved, and then oiled and polished to give a good finish. Shale panels were probably used as veneers. The sculptured remains show couches, complete with cushions and mattresses, with head and foot rests, either of the classical Greek backless type, or with the high back that was probably introduced by the Romans; chairs with continuous rounded

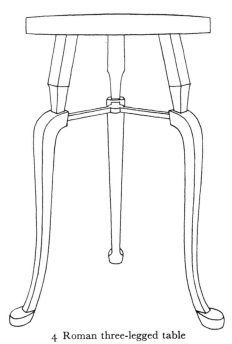

4 Roman three-legged table

Mediaeval Furniture

⸻

MEDIAEVAL furniture was limited in range and mostly of clumsy construction. It must be viewed against the roughness and insecurity of life in the primitive feudal society which succeeded Roman rule. Not until the end of the Middle Ages was there any development in comfort, and even then large houses were but sparsely furnished. In fact the word 'comfort' denoted strengthening or support and did not acquire its modern meaning until much later. The main furniture material was oak. The tree was first riven into quarters along the lines of the medullary rays with beetle and wedge, then cross-cut by saws, and finally dressed with adzes and planes. It was a tough, heavy, durable wood, easily obtainable from the dense forests, but inclined to move in the atmosphere and split, and unsuitable for delicate carving.

The furniture-making skills of the ancient world disappeared in the west with the Roman Empire and had to be slowly re-learnt. The earliest mediaeval craftsmen were the carpenter and blacksmith working in combination to produce rudimentary nailed furniture strengthened with strapwork. The wood carver, who worked mainly for the church, decorated furniture with Gothic tracery or with 'chip' carving, done with chisel and gouge. Another old craft was that of the turner, who was 'throwing' chairs at an early date. Later came the joiner who was responsible for panel and frame construction, and the cofferer who worked in wood but covered it with leather.

(1) To *c.* 1300

As early mediaeval furniture has entirely disappeared, we have to rely on sources such as illustrated manuscripts, literary references and sculpture for our scanty knowledge. To this day the chair retains something of the honorific value which it acquired when it was a rare piece of furniture reserved for important personages. The word 'cathedral' is taken from the *cathedra* or chair which was the bishop's throne. In castles and great houses only the head of the household sat in a chair, others occupying benches or stools. This was the procedure at the English court until the end of the Stuart period. The chairman of a committee meeting is still given the seat of authority, and the House of Commons contains only one chair—that of the Speaker who controls the proceedings—while all other members sit on benches. University professors occupy 'chairs', and prizewinners are sometimes chaired as a mark of honour.

The outstanding feature of the furniture of the period was its movability; much of it was designed to be transported from place to place, and to be easily dismantled, folded and packed up. The upper classes were constantly on the move. The king and his court, including his family, retainers and officials, travelled about the country dispensing government and justice, for there was no fixed capital until London began to assume that position in the fourteenth century. The royal household took with them their furniture, valuables and goods of all kinds, getting their food from the manors through which they passed, and from the great deer forests. Other landowners, lay and ecclesiastical, followed the same procedure on their estates; and in many European languages today the word for furniture is the same as for movables.

The nomadic character of mediaeval furniture explains the importance of the chest, the main piece, for it could be used not only for storing and transporting valuables and household goods, but also as a chair, table and bed. From it other pieces, such as settles, cabinets and chests of drawers, have developed. Early chests were of very primitive construction, merely hollowed-out tree trunks banded with iron for strength (hence the modern word 'trunk'). Later kinds were boarded (5),

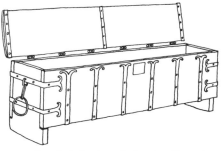

5 Boarded chest, early fourteenth century

i.e. built up of six massive boards or slabs pegged and nailed together, and made by the carpenter. Despite its clumsy appearance this kind was made until the seventeenth century (9), thin boards gradually replacing the slabs. But in the thirteenth

3

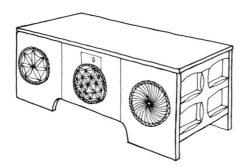

6 Joined chest, thirteenth century

century the joined chests also came into use (6, 10). The front was a single board tongued into grooves in the wide uprights or stiles, and joined with wooden pegs. These stiles were sometimes lengthened into feet and legs. In some cases the end boards were also tenoned or housed into the stiles and strengthened with cross-bars. The top at first had a wooden pin-hinge. These chests were decorated in various ways—chip carving (6), carved Gothic tracery (10), figures or scenes, inlay, painting or iron scrollwork. It seems certain that almost all of this early furniture, even when carved, was painted all over, no doubt to preserve it.

The centre of communal life in castle and manor house was the great hall, divided by a screen and minstrels' gallery from the kitchen quarters, and used by the lord and his retainers for eating and entertainment, and by the retainers for sleeping. The lord and his family had a smaller private room, the solar, above the hall. At meals the lord, his family and guests sat at the high table on a raised dais at one end of the hall, while dependants sat 'below the salt' in the body of the hall at trestle tables. The latter consisted of heavy oak or elm boards resting on supports (50). The tops could be lifted off after use and, with the trestles, stowed away to leave the hall clear. Thus 'board' meant a table, the sense retained in current phrases like 'bed and board' and 'board of directors'.

Though the chair was a rare piece, several types were in use. The chair of state, like a throne (11), and exemplified in the Coronation Chair in Westminster Abbey (7), was derived from the church choir stall, and had loose upholstery, the 'dorcer' (or 'dosser') on the back, and the 'banker' on the seat. Another kind was X-shaped and lighter in form. It was handier for transporting, and sometimes could be folded like a camp stool. The turned (or 'thrown') chair, a very old type, had a triangular seat, but the

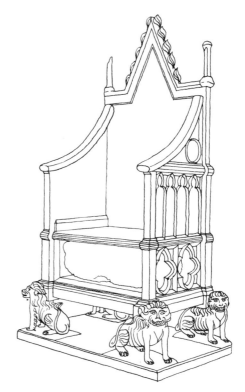

7 Coronation Chair

legs, arms, backs and supports were turned members (38).

The stool was the commonest seat, and for a long time was the name given to any kind of seat for one person. The tripod variety, with a round top and three legs, acquired very early its proverbial reputation for instability. The trestle kind had splayed uprights and an underframing for greater security (8). The popularity of the stool cannot be overstressed, for it was in constant demand until the chair came into general use at

8 Mediaeval trestle stool

4

9 The continuity of the chest; a boarded example of 1697

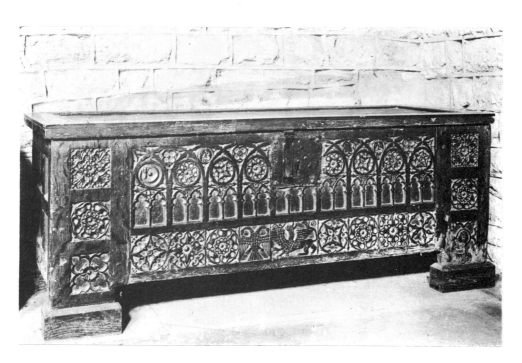

10 Joined chest of later mediaeval type with carved Gothic tracery

11 Canterbury Cathedral: Chair of
St. Augustine

12 Carved decoration on end of
panelled chest

the end of the seventeenth century (86), and even in the Georgian period chair-makers continued to make stools to match their sets of chairs. Among other seating furniture, settles and benches (or forms) (13) were really the same pieces, intended for several occupants, but settles were distinct in having arms. Some settles had boxes beneath their seats, showing how they had developed from chests. Settles and benches were usually placed against the walls of the great hall, sometimes being permanent fixtures, and trestle tables were set up before them at meal-times.

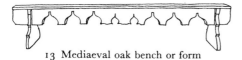

13 Mediaeval oak bench or form

From earliest times the most expensive piece of furniture was the bed. Its value, however, lay in its costly hangings, which were handed down as heirlooms, and not in its light wooden framework, for bedposts, back boards and cornices were not introduced until Tudor times. The canopy or tester was supported by cords from the ceiling. Only the richest households could afford several beds, which were placed about the house, as separate bedrooms were then unknown.

(2) c. 1300–1500

Towards the end of the mediaeval period social and economic conditions slowly encouraged the revival of domestic furniture. The growth of a merchant class was fostered by the development of the woollen industry and increasing trade with foreign countries. Town life began to flourish, politically through the grant of charters by the crown and nobility, economically through markets and fairs and the organisation of guilds to promote trade and craftsmanship. In the fourteenth century carpenters, joiners, turners and cofferers all formed separate guilds in London. The gradual decay of the feudal system and the decline of serfdom, and the extermination of the old aristocracy in the Wars of the Roses (1455–85) assured the importance of the mercantile middle class.

In the fifteenth century a notable advance was the development of the panelled chest (12, 14). A skeleton framework was built up of horizontal rails tenoned into vertical stiles at the top and bottom and secured by pegs, and panels were fitted into grooves in these rails and stiles. This was a real technical revolution. Not only was allowance now

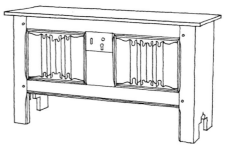

14 Panelled chest with linenfold decoration, early sixteenth century

made for the movement of the wood, but the chest, with lighter framework and sunken panels, was of more attractive appearance. 'Joined' furniture, or joinery, and with it the craft of the joiner, now became established. Panel and frame were a unit of design, applied in time to other pieces besides the chest, and to wainscoted walls; they meant lightness, strength and economy of material, and a sense of proportion. The principle is still widely used, as the importance of 'frame' in modern joinery indicates.

In the fifteenth century the joined chair (15), of box-like form derived from the chest, with panelled

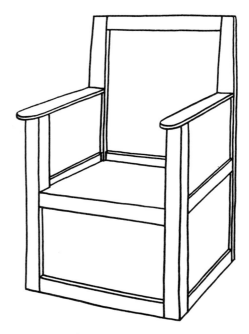

15 Joined chair, fifteenth century

back, sides and underframe, gradually came into use. Since the previous century the standing joined table with stretchers had been made; it was known as the table dormant to distinguish it from the demountable trestle table, though the latter continued to be the more usual kind. There were also gate-leg tables with folding tops ('faldyn' tables) and turned legs. In the great hall the serving or side table was developed from the chest; it was raised well off the floor and had carved panels. After the invention of printing, hanging shelves for books were found in some houses. The dresser, which had a long history behind it, and was originally a table on trestles for dressing meat before serving, now became a more ornate piece and was used for displaying plate.

Also used for the display of plate were 'cup-bordes', literally cup-boards or tables, open structures with shelves, for cups and vessels. They did not come to mean cupboards in the modern sense until later Tudor times. What we would call a cupboard was usually known at that time as an aumbry or press. An aumbry was originally a recess in the wall (and was used for storing books, among other things, in monasteries), and later an enclosed space with a door, or any small enclosed compartment in a larger piece of furniture. 'Cup-boards with aumbries' obviously refer to the latter, and were cup-boards with enclosed spaces beneath the top. The aumbry probably acquired its early meaning of receptacle from its use for storing food for distribution to the poor, under the direction of the almoner. The press was for linen and clothes.

Furniture decoration continued mainly on traditional lines, but another fifteenth-century innovation was the carved linenfold pattern, probably of Flemish origin, on panelled furniture and woodwork (14, 16, 22, 25). Its name came from its supposed resemblance to folded linen.

Though some of the larger English houses now began to resemble comfortable homes, they lagged far behind Flanders in this respect. Flemish furniture, particularly 'Flaunders chests', was imported here, so much so that in 1483 Richard III imposed a short-lived ban on the trade in response to protests from English cofferers.

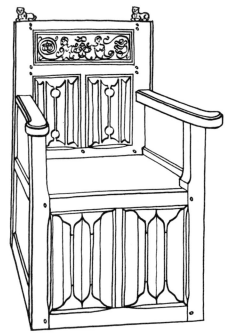

16 Joined chair with linenfold panelling, mid-sixteenth century

Flemish craftsmen also came to England to make furniture.

The most important English craftsman in the late mediaeval period was the cofferer. Originally the maker of articles for travel and transport, including travelling trunks known as trussing coffers (or standards), he slowly enlarged the scope of his craft to make not only coffers and chests (these two terms were largely interchangeable at the time) but also chairs, stools, screens, small jewel coffers and desks. He used wood basically, but covered it with leather and, later, with a variety of fine materials such as velvet and cloth-of-gold. By 1500 he was the chief court furniture craftsman, and indeed figured among royal craftsmen until the end of the Georgian period, still making chests and similar pieces for storage and transport.

The Tudor Period

1485–1603

---◇---

In spite of the domestic discontent caused by religious changes, enclosures and inflation, and of threats from foreign enemies (e.g. the Armada 1588), the Tudor government ended baronial misrule, ensured internal stability and increased England's prestige abroad. Although the country played at first only a minor role in the geographical discoveries, her growing overseas trade steadily advanced her wealth. There was a vigour in national life which was particularly marked in the reign of Elizabeth I (1558–1603). The Italian Renaissance began to make its influence felt under Henry VII (1485–1509) and Henry VIII (1509–47) but its classical forms were not really understood by English craftsmen and were at first mixed incongruously with traditional Gothic ornament.

The Reformation greatly affected domestic life. After Henry VIII's break with Rome (Act of Supremacy 1534, and dissolution of the monasteries, 1536–9) Italian cultural influence was replaced by that of Protestant Germany and the Netherlands. A new class of landowners, created by the sale of monastic estates, strongly upheld the Reformation settlement and exploited their lands for profit, building new houses with the proceeds, or modernising their old ones. Building activity was now centred on private houses, and no longer on churches. Thus conditions favoured the increased output of furniture, which was rapidly changing its forms.

Tudor wills and inventories (such as the inventory of Henry VIII's furniture in 1547) reveal clearly the variety of pieces of furniture now found in great houses, but confusion still exists about some of their names and uses, as they are not always described precisely, though they were naturally familiar to contemporaries. Old names were kept for new articles; other pieces, in use then, have now disappeared, and their exact function is uncertain. The confusion is made worse by the habit of modern dealers of giving unauthorised names (e.g. refectory table, monk's bench and bible box) to Tudor pieces.

(1) Early Tudor
(1485–1558)

The new developments in furniture were at first imposed on the traditional pattern of life. When Henry VIII enlarged Hampton Court, begun by Cardinal Wolsey in 1515, he built the Great Hall (1531–6) in the mediaeval style. Here, as in other large houses of the time, the Renaissance made its influence felt in modes of decoration rather than in building style. The hall in English houses was still separated by a screen and passage from the kitchen and other domestic offices. But at the upper end of the hall were now more private rooms for the family, the parlour or sitting-room, closets and bedrooms. The servants slept in the pantry or buttery, in the attics or above the stables. Meals were still taken by the whole household in the hall.

As in mediaeval times, a large chair was reserved in a conspicuous position on the dais in the hall for the master, as a symbol of his status (16). Other kinds of chairs, joined, turned and X-shaped, were becoming more plentiful, though stools, settles and forms remained the usual seating furniture. A lighter type of joined chair, the *caquetoire*, was found in parlours and bedrooms, and was based on French types; it had a narrow back and widely splayed arms, and was open beneath the arms and seat (17). Its name is said to have come from its use as a conversation chair (French, *caqueter*, to chatter). Another kind of seat was the table-chair or table-bench (wrongly called a 'monk's bench'), the back of which was hinged so that it could be turned forward to form a table top when required (18, 44).

Among tables, the chief was the high table or table dormant in the hall. The trestle table, however, was still widely used. One version had the top supported on strong oak or elm uprights which were united by rails and stretchers secured by oak pegs outside the uprights; once the pegs were removed, rails, stretchers, uprights and top could all be easily stored (19). About 1550 the draw-leaf table made its appearance; the two smaller leaves beneath the top could be drawn

9

17 Armchair, caquetoire type

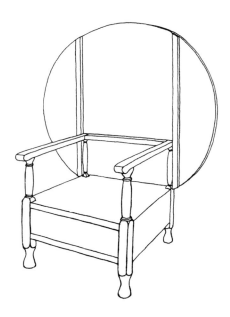

18 Table-chair of traditional form, early seventeenth century

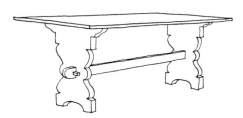

19 Tudor trestle table

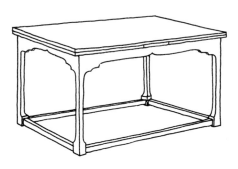

20 Early Tudor draw-leaf table

out to extend the table to almost double its length (20). Smaller tables were now found scattered about the house, used for a variety of purposes, and among them was the games table, which had a folding top and a small compartment in the upper part for dice. The hutch table, used as a side table, had a long, narrow top with a cupboard underneath, and was raised on short legs (21).

While cup-boards still preserved their traditional meaning of open-shelved pieces for display, they were also gradually beginning to acquire something of their modern sense of doored structures. References in inventories to 'close' cup-boards, and to 'cup-boards with aumbries' indicated wholly or partly enclosed pieces. Other doored receptacles included the large press for clothes and linen, the livery cup-board, and the

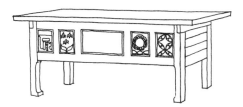

21 Early Tudor oak side table

hutch, a term of wide meaning which included a roughly made chest or, as here, a more ornamental piece raised on legs and with one or more doors (22). A feature of the livery (or dole) cupboard was the pierced Gothic tracery in the doors to provide ventilation, as it was used for storing

22 Oak linenfold hutch, 1500

the food needed for daily distribution to the members of a large household. A well-known example, said to have belonged to Henry VII's eldest son, is dated about 1500 (23).

It was at this time that the great bed began to acquire its heavy wooden framework of four carved posts and panelled back board. The canopy was still suspended from the ceiling, but about 1550 it began to be replaced by a solid tester which rested on the two front posts (which stood clear from the bedstock, i.e. the wooden frame for the bedding) and on the back board (the two rear posts now being discarded). The truckle bed, a low bed on wheels, was used by the personal servants of the master and pushed under the great bed when not required.

The carved ornament on early Tudor furniture which showed traces of Italian Renaissance influence, took the form of roundels with human heads in profile ('Romayne' decoration) (25)

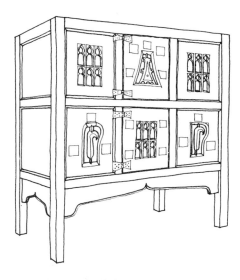

23 'Prince Arthur's Cupboard' carved with the Prince of Wales' feathers and the letter A, c. 1500

and other classical motives, freely mixed with Gothic tracery, linenfold and the Tudor Rose (24). Much of this furniture was painted or gilded. This is explained, apart from the love of bright and gay interiors, by the need to protect furniture

24 Tudor Rose and tracery panel from sideboard (from H. Shaw 1836)

from the weather, as window glass was rare until the end of the century. Oak panelling on the walls, plasterwork on the ceilings, and tapestry carpets for wall hangings and table covers, formed the background for this furniture.

(2) Elizabethan
(1558–1603)

Significant changes in both housing and furnishing occurred in this period. Many Elizabethan houses were built in plan like the letter H

25 Early Tudor close cupboard with 'Romayne' and linenfold decoration

26 'Nonesuch' chest of Elizabethan period; so called from supposed resemblance of inlaid decoration to Henry VIII's Palace of Nonesuch, Cheam

27 Oak armchair with folding framework, c. 1600

28

28 Elizabethan court cup-board

29 Early seventeenth-century cupboard showing typical inlaid and carved decoration

29

30 Elizabethan strapwork and leaf design
(from H. Shaw 1836)

or half-H, and the great hall, now only one storey high, began to lose its importance, leaving more room for the development of the parlour, great chamber and long gallery. The latter, an Elizabethan innovation, was used for family gatherings, musical entertainments, dancing, and, especially in winter months when bad weather often made the roads impassable, for exercise.

31 Elizabethan arabesque strapwork
(from H. Shaw 1836)

With the decline of Italian influence, exuberant Flemish and German decoration, copied from imported pattern-books which the invention of printing now made readily available, was much used on furniture after 1550. This took the form of strapwork, i.e. interlaced geometrical and arabesque ornament carved in low relief (30, 31, 35) and of arcading of semicircular Roman arches (27).

32 Elizabethan egg and dart design
(from H. Shaw 1836)

The vitality of the age was also seen in the elaborately carved 'bulbs' which were prepared in sections and glued to bedposts, table legs and cupboard supports, reflecting the puffed sleeves and trunks of contemporary costume (28, 33, 34). More and more, furniture became a prized personal possession and was often carved with the owner's initials and dated.

33 Elizabethan walnut court cupboard,
c. 1590

The painting of furniture went out of fashion with the more general use of glass windows, and was replaced by inlay in floral or chequer patterns (26, 28), worked in contrasting colours with bog oak, holly and ebony, and by the wider employment of upholstery on chairs and stools; or the surfaces were left plain and either waxed or varnished.

34 Walnut bedstead carved and inlaid with
holly and bogwood, 1593

Tapestries from the Netherlands, Turkey carpets (from the Levant) for tablecloths and cushions, and squab cushions of velvet, silk and cloth of gold or silver, all showed the growing wealth from trade and the fondness for colourful

15

35 Part of Charles I headboard of bedstead
(from H. Shaw 1836)

interiors. The joiners made freer use of walnut, birch, cedar, fir and chestnut, though oak kept its fashionable lead.

Upholstered seating furniture was gradually becoming more fashionable. Some elaborate X-shaped chairs were produced by the coffer-makers, and by 1600 this type was fully upholstered and had scrolled arms which projected beyond the uprights (36). The joined chair became lighter in construction but was often floridly decorated with carved scrolled cresting on the top and brackets at each side; there was either carving or inlay on the back and on the edge of the seat. The panelled side beneath the arms, however, had now gone, and by the end of Elizabeth's reign the panels

37 Elizabethan joined chair, c. 1600

beneath the seat had also disappeared, leaving an open frame and turned legs connected by stretchers (37). At this time, too, a number of

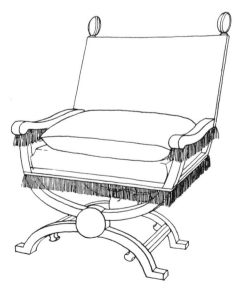

36 Elizabethan X-frame armchair, c. 1600

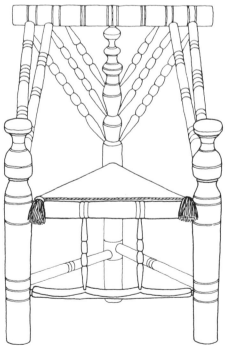

38 Turned or 'thrown' chair of traditional form, first half of seventeenth century

chairs of the lighter, more movable, *caquetoire* type, with widely-splayed arms, were made. The traditional 'thrown' chair long persisted, with its triangular seat and highly decorative turning (38). A new type of chair with folding framework was introduced about 1600 (27). After 1550 the joined stool, with four turned legs, gradually became more popular than the old trestle type (39).

41 Portable oak desk, *c.* 1590

made the convenient draw-leaf table popular, especially for dining parlours (40).

Some Elizabethan beds were the largest and most elaborate structures of their kind ever seen in England, with heavily carved bulbous foot posts and massive panelled back boards ornamented with carving and inlay (34). The biggest and most famous of all was the Great Bed of Ware, made at the end of the century, and mentioned by Shakespeare and other writers of the time. Such beds, of course, were the possessions of rich people, but that the standard of comfort was now beginning to affect other classes is indicated by Harrison's reference in 1587 to the increased use of joined beds and feather mattresses by artificers and farmers.

39 Elizabethan joined stool

An Elizabethan piece was the court cup-board (from the French *court*, 'short', as it was rarely more than four feet high), a three-tiered open sideboard for displaying plate (28, 33). A closely related type to this had an enclosed compartment in the upper stage, which was either straight fronted or splayed (52); or, again, in another variation, known as a press cupboard, the lower stage was also enclosed by two large doors (29, 53). This last kind was a cupboard in the modern sense.

Though the long joined and trestle (50) tables of traditional form continued to be made, the gradual replacement of the communal life of the great hall by the increasing use of private rooms

42 Elizabethan cot

The smaller size of printed books, and the need for suitable writing furniture, led to the greater production of portable desks, of the kind used in the mediaeval period. They were of box form, for storing books and writing materials, and had hinged, sloping tops with ledges. They could be stood on tables and were forerunners of bureaux (41). They are often wrongly called bible-boxes.

40 Elizabethan draw-leaf table, *c.* 1600

The Early Stuart Period
1603–1660

———◇———

THE early Stuart period, including the reigns of James I (1603–25), from whom the term Jacobean is derived, and of Charles I (1625–49), and the period of the Commonwealth (1649–60), was the last great phase of fashionable oak furniture. Classical Renaissance architecture on Italian models was introduced by Inigo Jones, the Surveyor-General to both James I and Charles I. He followed the simple and elegant classicism of Andrea Palladio (1517–80), the leading architect of the later Italian Renaissance, in his two major buildings, the Banqueting Hall, Whitehall (1619–21) and the Queen's House, Greenwich (1619–35). So slight had been Italian influence under the Tudors that the re-appearance of true classical forms amounted to a real revolution, but Jones's work, in spite of the encouragement of Charles I, the most cultured of English monarchs, was hampered by the king's lack of money and was stopped altogether by the outbreak of the Civil War in 1642.

The quarrel between king and parliament tended to curtail the building and furnishing of larger houses. The temper of the times favoured more sober decoration on furniture, and the excessive ornament of the Elizabethan period was gradually toned down, a development which was encouraged by the austere Puritanism of Cromwell's rule after 1649.

In London, now rapidly becoming the chief furniture-making centre of the country, there was growing specialisation among craftsmen. In 1632, after a long dispute over the demarcation of their crafts, the London guilds of joiners and carpenters came to an agreement which in effect gave the joiners the monopoly of making furniture involving the use of mortises and tenons, frames and dovetails. This agreement was not always kept, and applied only to London, but the supremacy of the joiner's skill was no longer in doubt. In particular, chair-making became a specialised branch of joinery, and for generations the royal joiners were to make chairs of state for the crown. These chairs were finished by the upholsterers, who thus gradually ousted the coffer-makers.

Richly upholstered chairs and stools of the Elizabethan type continued to be made at first in the early seventeenth century in great houses. Some fine X-shaped chairs had the whole of their woodwork covered with fringed velvet, silk, satin and other expensive materials, which were fastened to the frames by brass-headed nails (43). Of a simpler kind were the first single chairs (or 'back-stools', i.e. without arms) to be made in this country. Among them were 'farthingale' chairs (47), to accommodate ladies wearing the fashionable extravagantly hooped skirts of the time. These chairs had padded seats and backs, the latter being raised well clear of the seats. Their legs and stretchers were plain, some legs being of columnar form. They were often upholstered with cheaper materials such as Turkey work (wool on a canvas base, imitating Turkey carpets) and leather. Upholstered chairs were often of beech or walnut, but the old type of joined chairs, with open arms and panelled backs, were usually of oak. They were destined to have a long life still before them, especially in country areas. At this time their back panels were frequently arched and inlaid with a variety of woods. About 1650 lighter types of chairs, in addition to the panel-backs, were made by north-country craftsmen and are known as Yorkshire and Derbyshire chairs. Their backs were formed either of an arcading of turned balusters on a central rail (48), or of two broad and flat hooped rails. At about the same time appeared some austerely designed chairs with backs and seats covered with leather fastened by brass studs, and with knob-turned legs and stretchers (49).

Where space permitted families to continue the practice of dining in the hall, the immovable long joined tables and the larger kind of draw-leaf tables remained in active use. Those made in this period gradually discarded the exaggerated bulbous legs, which were now of simple baluster form, or fluted. But inevitably the need for easily-moved side tables increased, and nearly all large houses had gate-legged tables. Tables with folding tops had been in use since the fifteenth century, but now the gate principle of pivoted legs, connected

43

43 X-frame armchair covered in velvet used by James I

45 Oak cupboard, *c.* 1625 showing guilloche
decoration

45

44 Early Stuart table-chair

46 Mid-seventeenth-century oak chest in
two halves for easy transportation enclosing
drawers

46

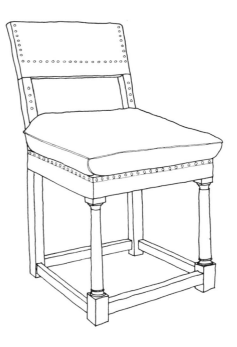

47 Walnut Farthingale chair, early seventeenth century

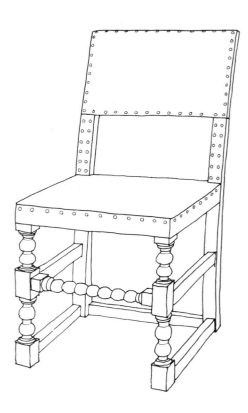

49 Turned oak chair covered in leather, *c.* 1650

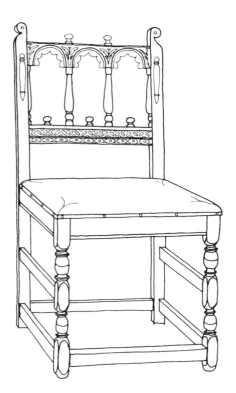

48 Turned and carved oak chair, Yorkshire-Derbyshire type, mid-seventeenth century

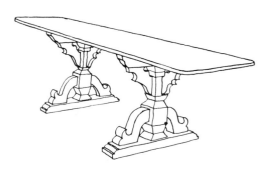

50 Oak trestle dining-table, 1610

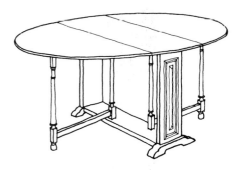

51 Gate-legged table, first half of seventeenth century

53 Press cupboard, carved oak with inlay. Marriage initials A.M. and date, 1610

by stretchers to the top and bottom of the table, was widely developed. Some of these tables had a carved arcaded underframing. The tops were sometimes folded with one flap, hinged in the middle, sometimes with two flaps (and two gates). A number of the latter had trestle type ends with shaped feet linked by a stretcher (51).

By this time cupboards were acquiring their modern meaning (45), but open-shelved three-tiered court cup-boards were still being made, as well as the partly enclosed hall and parlour cupboards (52). Some fine examples of the wholly enclosed press cupboard were also made (29, 53). In addition to their turned supports (instead of bulbs) they were often decorated with lozenges (54), lunettes (55), fluting (56) and guilloches (45, 57), and with split balusters applied to their surfaces (59). These pieces were slowly going out of fashion in larger houses, but they continued

in smaller ones until much later. Food cupboards were also still in use; Gothic tracery in their doors was now replaced by turned spindles, and some smaller varieties were hung against the wall. Among other pieces of the same kind were the bread cupboard with a sloping top (58) (a traditional type which was also loosely known as a hutch, and in the north of England as an ark), and the newer form of chest enclosing drawers, marking the transition towards the chest of drawers (46, 59).

54 Lozenge decoration

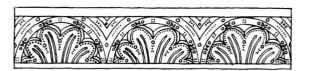

55 Lunette decoration (from H. Shaw 1836)

52 Court cupboard, early seventeenth century

56 Fluting (from H. Shaw 1836)

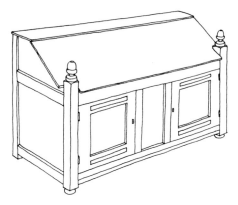

58 Bread cupboard ('ark'), early seventeenth century

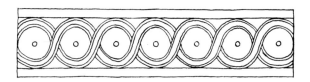

57 Guilloche

59 Chest enclosing drawers, early seventeenth century

The Later Stuart Period

1660–1714

(1) The Walnut Period

The Restoration of Charles II in 1660 saw the beginning of a revolution in the decoration, design and variety of English furniture largely because England was opened to the full impact of foreign ideas which were rapidly assimilated by English craftsmen. Growing wealth through trade and colonisation, success in war, first against the Dutch and then against the French, and the foundation of the Bank of England in 1694 all combined to make England, by the end of this period, the leading commercial, colonial and financial power of Europe. The rich merchant class vied with the landowning aristocracy for improved standards of comfort and elegance. The Great Fire of London in 1666 gave Sir Christopher Wren his golden opportunity to rebuild St Paul's and over fifty City churches in a national version of the classical style, which now spread rapidly. His work for the Crown at Hampton Court, Greenwich and elsewhere was to have a profound influence on domestic architecture generally. London, where there was now an unprecedented demand for furniture, could readily import the finest timbers and upholstery materials from abroad, and became indisputably the country's chief furniture centre.

Walnut was the fashionable furniture wood for almost a century after 1660, supreme until about 1725, then, until 1750, gradually yielding its place to mahogany. Two varieties were used, the *juglans regia* (light brown in colour) and the *juglans nigra* (dark brown with strong markings). Both kinds were grown in England, but insufficiently to meet the demand, and there were considerable imports of the former from the Continent and of the latter from Virginia. European walnut, especially that from Grenoble in France, had a more decorative figure than English walnut, and its high cost encouraged its use as a veneer, a process already well established abroad. Thin, saw-cut sheets of the wood were glued to carefully prepared surfaces of carcase wood, which was usually yellow deal imported from the Baltic. The panel and frame construction

of oak furniture was useless for this new method as it did not provide a flush surface, and oak was unsuitable for carcases as its movement tended to unsettle veneers glued to it. Thus veneering represented a technical revolution of the same magnitude as the introduction of panelled furniture in the fifteenth century, and it, too, required a new kind of specialist craftsman—the cabinet-maker. It is probable that this new technique was brought here by immigrant foreign craftsmen who taught it to English workers. The latter picked it up quickly, for shortly after 1660 the term cabinet-maker came into regular use.

The great attraction of walnut was its variety of beautiful figures. Veneers cut from the same piece of wood repeated its figure, so that symmetrical patterns laid together on pieces of furniture had a highly decorative effect, and were often enclosed by cross-banded borders with a narrow inner edging of herringbone pattern (60). Besides walnut,

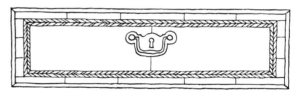

60 Drawer front showing half round moulding, cross banding and herringbone banding

other finely-figured woods were used as veneers, particularly in the earlier part of this period. Among them were ash, elm, mulberry, yew, maple, laburnum and, above all, olive and princes wood (now called kingwood). Interesting figures were crotches (cut from junction of branch and trunk), circular and oval oyster-pieces (cut transversely from small branches) and burrs (excrescences on the trunk, producing irregular and intricate veins). Walnut was also used in the solid, for it had an admirable texture and carved well; its one serious defect was its liability to attack by worm.

A special form of veneering was known as marquetry. This term had been used earlier in the century to describe inlay, but it was now more

61 Charles II period table with double gates

62 Painted side table and torchère (candle-stand)
c. 1685, with twist turning.

63 Detail of carved 'Boyes and Crownes' decoration on front stretcher
of chair dated 1687

64 Charles II scrutoire decorated with parquetry

properly applied to the technique, again introduced from abroad, of cutting veneers of many different coloured woods into patterns and fitting them together on a veneer ground, like a jig-saw puzzle. For this purpose woods were chosen for their colour, and not their figure, and were, if necessary, dyed, stained, bleached or scorched in hot sand to get the right shade. Sycamore, for instance was stained greenish-grey and widely used under the name of harewood. Floral marquetry was in fashion until about 1700, at first in bright colours and then, about 1690, in quieter shades of browns and golds. After 1700 arabesque (or 'seaweed') marquetry (88), an English style in intricate patterns of two contrasting woods, one dark and one light, became popular. Similar in technique to marquetry was parquetry (64), the arrangement of oyster-pieces in geometrical designs; olive was often used for this, its dark greenish tinge being frequently relieved by inlaid lines of boxwood.

This period also saw the growing influence of oriental designs and decoration on English furniture. Trade with the Far East through the East India Company (founded 1600) had already introduced lacquer furniture into England, but after 1660 much greater quantities were imported and sold in 'Indian' shops. English merchants also shipped models of our furniture to the East

to be copied and lacquered there and re-imported. This aroused protests from English craftsmen who had begun to make their own versions of lacquer furniture, and in 1700 they successfully petitioned Parliament to cripple this trade by high import duties, and thus keep the home market for English imitations. The latter, however, never achieved the beautiful colour and finish of oriental work, and it is important to distinguish lacquer, the genuine oriental decoration, from japanning, its English counterpart, which was similar to varnishing.

The social habits and interests of the upper classes in this period were reflected in new types of furniture. The craze for gambling led to card tables, and the increase in letter writing (through improved postal services) to varied kinds of writing furniture. Rich men's collections of curiosities (or 'rarities'), usually small valuable objects like medals, coins and jewels, were kept in specially designed cabinets. The production of clocks of all kinds was stimulated by the vastly improved accuracy of timekeeping, one of the notable results of the interest in science which was promoted by the incorporation of the Royal Society in 1662.

(2) Charles II
(1660–1685)

The Restoration of 1660 marked a reaction against eleven years of Puritan rule. A love of flamboyant decoration was inspired by the example of Charles II and his luxury-loving court, who had seen the best of European craftsmanship during their exile abroad. The chief foreign influences came from France which, under Louis XIV, was rapidly becoming Europe's artistic leader, and from Holland. Turning, carving, marquetry, parquetry and lacquer all illustrated the current desire for ornamental, rich-looking furniture.

To speed the rebuilding of London after the Great Fire a standard plan was adopted for new houses, which were now made of brick and stone and no longer of wood. There were an entrance hall and staircase with two or three rooms and a closet on each floor, the number of storeys varying from two to four, plus a garret in each case, according to the class of house. Parlours, eating-rooms and bed chambers, with painted pine panelling on the walls, moulded plaster ceilings, and carved pine fireplaces, were the settings for the new furniture.

25

Shortly after 1660 cane furniture was introduced from abroad. It had the advantages of being light, clean, cheap and durable, and chairs, stools and daybeds were made with walnut frames and cane seats and backs, sometimes in matching suites. Cane chairs at first resembled in shape the leather-padded chairs of the Cromwellian period, but with coarse-meshed cane instead of leather in the backs and seats, and twist-turned instead of bobbin-turned frames (65). Later, more ornate kinds appeared. The more expensive ones had high, narrow backs with twist-turned uprights, a carved back panel for the cane work, a carved cresting tenoned between the uprights, and a wide front stretcher rail carved to match the cresting (66). Typical decoration on this elaborate carving, which was frequently pierced, including cupids supporting a crown ('Boyes and Crownes') (63), flowers and foliage. There was much scroll work on the back panels, arms and front legs. The best chairs were of walnut, but cheaper kinds were of beech, stained or japanned. Cane chairs had a long vogue. They seem to have been made only in London, and, adapted to changing styles, were manufactured until well into the eighteenth century. Closely related to chairs were daybeds or couches which

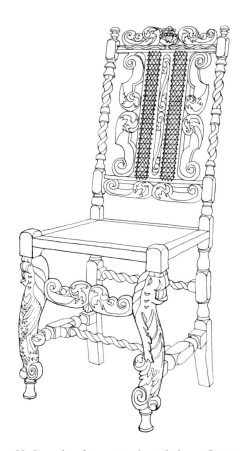

66 Carved and turned walnut chair, c. 1670–5

were used by the well-to-do for reclining in the living rooms, where there were no longer beds. They had raked cane back-rests like chair backs, though squatter in form, and long cane seats supported on six or more legs joined by richly carved stretchers (67). Upholstered easy chairs with wings (as protection from draughts) had low backs and padded arms and were covered with rich materials like damask, silk and velvet which often ended in fringes. Similar in covering and structure were winged settees, usually composed of two or three chair backs combined together.

With the development of separate eating-rooms, the old draw-leaf tables went out of fashion, and were replaced by oval or circular gate-legged tables with two flaps (61). In larger houses several of these tables were used, as they could be conveniently folded and removed after meals, leaving plenty of clear floor space. Equally convenient were small tables which stood in the various rooms, serving a number of purposes. They had twist-turned legs joined by flat stretchers (62, 68) and were usually decorated with oyster-pieces of

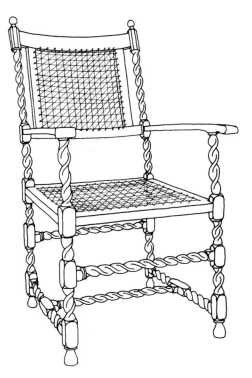

65 Turned walnut cane chair, c. 1665

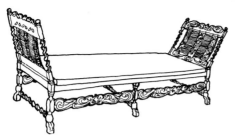

67 Daybed of walnut, *c.* 1670

68 Small Charles II table

idea copied from abroad. These stands, which often had a long single drawer, had twist-turned legs joined by flat veneered stretchers or, after about 1680, scrolled legs. The chest was at last beginning to lose its long-established popularity as the chest of drawers gradually took its place. The latter was usually made with five drawers, three long ones at the bottom and two shallower ones at the top; it was not a tall piece, even on its stand, and the top drawer could be easily reached (70). The drawer fronts made excellent grounds for fine figured veneers, with cross-banding and herring-bone edging. Their decorative effect was increased by the half-round moulding which was applied to the rails between the drawers, and which was commonly used until about 1700.

Scrutoires were the earliest writing cabinets. They were box-like pieces on stands, and had numerous small drawers and pigeon holes for letters, and a large fall-front which, when opened, provided a flat writing surface (64, 71). But small writing desks, of traditional form, with interior compartments, still remained in general use; they were very handy, and could be stood on tables.

For their collections of curiosities the upper classes used cabinets on stands. These were very

walnut, olive and laburnum, or with marquetry. Those obviously designed to stand against the wall were decorated on three sides only. A very popular and attractive arrangement of the time was that of 'a Table, Glass and Stands'—a side table standing beneath a looking-glass and flanked by a pair of candle stands, to give maximum light (62). This grouping served as a dressing-table.

Mirrors were slowly coming into more general use; they were still expensive but looking-glass plate was now being made at the Duke of Buckingham's glass works at Vauxhall, and for the first time it was no longer necessary to depend on foreign (mainly Venetian) imports. These early mirrors were oblong or square in shape and had broad frames of half-round section, sometimes surmounted by a semicircular hood (69). The decoration of the frames, e.g. veneers, marquetry, japanning, and their material (some were made of silver) received special attention owing to their importance in the interior.

At this time many of the new types of case furniture, such as chests of drawers, scrutoires (the English name for the French *escritoires*), cabinets and bureaux, were mounted on stands, another

69 Charles II mirror

70 Walnut chest of drawers on stand,
late seventeenth century

71 Charles II scrutoire showing open
fall-front

72 Bracket clock, late seventeenth century

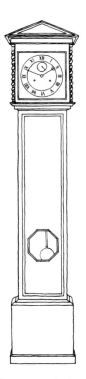

73 Long-case clock, c. 1680

similar in their appearance, and in the arrangement of their interiors, to scrutoires, except that they had a pair of folding doors. Many scrutoires and cabinets were richly decorated with marquetry and parquetry on the fall-fronts and doors, and on the fronts of the small drawers inside. Their tops were usually flat and had moulded cornices, beneath which were pulvinated (or 'swell') friezes made to pull out as drawers. Many gorgeously-coloured lacquered cabinets were also imported from the Far East and imitated by English japanners. They had prominent engraved hinges and elaborate lock plates, and were often mounted on ornate gilt or silvered stands with deep aprons (76).

The introduction of the pendulum gave clocks an accuracy never achieved before, and they became part of every well-furnished house. Short (or 'bob') pendulums were enclosed in bracket or table clocks, which were surmounted by a handle so that they could be easily carried from room to room (72). About 1670 Robert Hooke invented the long (or 'royal') pendulum of 39.1 in., which took a second over each swing, and the anchor escapement, which controlled the clock's mechanism so that the pendulum swung in a small arc. These were incorporated into long-case clocks, with a hood for the movement and dial, a tall narrow case for the pendulum, and a pedestal base (73). While the clock-makers concentrated on the mechanism, the specialist clock-case-makers made the cases, which were often decorated with marquetry. English clock-making now entered on its golden age, and some clock-makers, Thomas Tompion among whom was outstanding, achieved a European reputation.

In an entry in his diary in 1666 Samuel Pepys refers to what are probably the earliest domestic bookcases which can be given a definite date (74). He engaged 'Simpson the joiner' to make 'presses' for his numerous books. Twelve of these bookcases are still preserved at Magdalene College, Cambridge. Made of oak, they have glazed doors in both their tall upper sections and their lower bases. Bookcases of similar design were made for the rapidly-growing libraries of large houses.

Wealthy households continued to spend large sums on beds, particularly on the state beds reserved for important visitors. The whole of the framework, including the slender posts, was now covered with costly materials and often stretched up to the ceiling, its height increased by finials of ostrich plumes at the four corners of the tester.

74 Oak bookcase made for Samuel Pepys

Such beds, like so many other pieces of the period, vividly illustrate Evelyn's words written at the death of Charles II: 'He brought in a politer way of living, which passed to luxury and intolerable expense'.

(3) William and Mary
(1689–1702)

The accession of William and Mary, after the expulsion of James II, brought on the whole a quieter touch into English furniture and decoration. This was due in part to the more formal atmosphere at court under 'Dutch William' (who reigned alone after Mary's death in 1694) and in part to the natural English tendency to tone down extravagant forms. More immigrant craftsmen reached England, first the French Huguenots who fled here after the revocation of the Edict of Nantes in 1685, including both skilled marquetry workers and the silk weavers who established the Spitalfields silk industry, and second, Dutch cabinet-makers who came over with William, some of them as court craftsmen. One of the most influential designers was Daniel Marot, a Huguenot who had already taken refuge at

75 William and Mary dressing-table

75

76 Oriental cabinet on carved and gilt
stand, *c.* 1700

76

77 Desk and bookcase japanned in red and gold, *c.* 1700

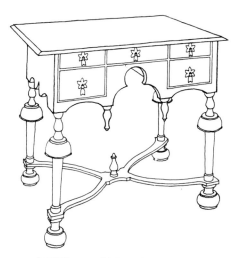

78 William and Mary dressing-table
with 'peg' baluster legs

William's court in Holland and now visited England. He produced many designs for interiors and furniture which were closely related to the contemporary Louis XIV style, and owed much to Bérain and Lepautre, two outstanding French designers.

Both marquetry and turning illustrated the tendency towards less exuberant decoration. The bright floral designs of early marquetry became quieter shades of browns and golds about 1690, and at the same time arabesque (or 'seaweed') was coming into fashion. The latter had intricate patterns but only two shades of colour, a light one (box, holly, sycamore or pear) for the design, and walnut for the darker background (88). The complex designs were based on the marquetry in metal and tortoiseshell which Boulle and his followers were producing in France. Twist-turning on the legs of furniture gradually gave way to scrolls and baluster turning in a variety of attractive forms, of which the best known is the peg (or bell) top (78). These legs ended on feet of many varied shapes—bun, ball, hoof, scroll and square.

The chairs of this period are noted for their tall and slender backs, of graceful proportions, which were partly designed for ladies wearing the fashionable high hair styles. The arched cresting (still often matching the front stretchers) now rested on the uprights instead of being tenoned between them (79). Scrolled front legs were still being made, but straight legs were coming into vogue, either baluster turned or square and tapering. Some chairs dispensed with the carved

front stretcher and instead had a curved **X**-shaped stretcher which met in a central finial. The backs were filled with cane (now of very fine mesh) or with carved foliage and scroll work. Their pronounced backward rake, and the dowel jointing of the cresting to the uprights and of the front legs to the seat (or to the arm supports in the case of arm-chairs) resulted in a certain amount of structural weakness. Upholstered chairs without arms (80), having the same kind of tall, rectangular, raked backs, were covered with rich materials and often had their woodwork gilded. Upholstered wing arm-chairs (81) and settees kept very much to their earlier forms, but now often with baluster legs and curved stretchers.

The earliest tables designed specially for card playing and for writing made their appearance. Cards had hitherto been played on any convenient small table. Now veneered walnut card tables were made with oval or circular folding tops and baluster or tapered legs, two of which swung out to support the flap. Writing tables were very

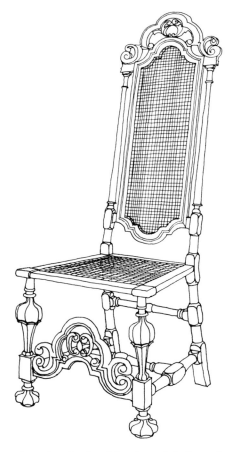

79 Carved and painted beechwood chair, c. 1690–5

32

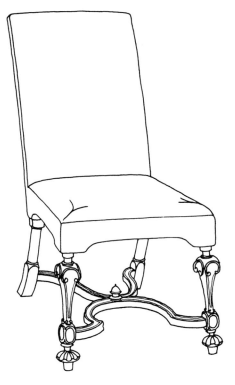

80 Upholstered walnut chair, *c.* 1690

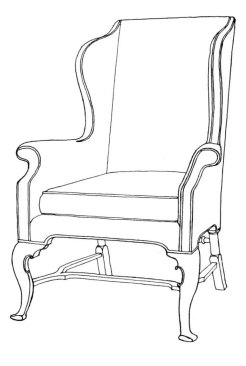

81 Walnut wing chair covered with needlework, *c.* 1700

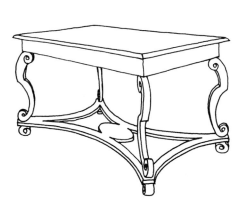

82 William and Mary side table with scrolled legs

83 Small walnut bureau on stand, *c.* 1700

similar except that they had rectangular folding flaps and were often decorated with marquetry. Another kind of table, for dressing, had a number of small drawers for brushes, combs, etc. (75, 78).

Ornamental side tables, decorated also with marquetry or japan, became more and more imposing in appearance, with S-scrolled legs and curved stretchers (82). Many had their tops covered with gesso, a composition of parchment size and chalk which was laid on like plaster, carved and gilded (or, more rarely, silvered). Some of the more elaborated gilt side tables were obviously inspired by French influence, following the designs of Bérain and Marot, and were no doubt made by French craftsmen living in England.

The scrutoire remained in favour but for steadier support it was mounted on a chest of drawers instead of a stand. It had, however, one serious disadvantage in that there was no room for papers when the fall-front was closed, and thus the bureau, which had a sloping front and a convenient space for papers, began to replace it. These early bureaux were on stands (83) and of narrow width so that they could be placed against the wall between the windows. Cabinets were also changing. Those fitted with small drawers were now decorated with arabesque marquetry, and their tops had arched pediments in a variety of forms. In some cases, a chest of drawers was used as a stand. Oriental-style cabinets, decorated with japan, were supported on ornate gilt or silvered stands some of which resembled Marot's side tables (76). Another type of cabinet had glazed doors and an interior fitted with shelves to display china. This was a fashion inspired by Queen Mary, who brought back from Holland a fine collection of oriental porcelain and Delftware which she displayed at Hampton Court (some of it is still there). For this purpose, shelves were also made above chimney pieces, and the practice of setting pieces of china about the house spread rapidly. China cabinets, however, were rare before 1700.

Interest in the appearance and comfort of the home was everywhere increasing. Much of the japanning of furniture was done by the owners themselves at home, for a veritable craze for this kind of decoration followed the publication in 1688 of Stalker and Parker's *Treatise of Japanning and Varnishing*, a practical handbook on gilding, lacquering and decorative painting 'for the splendour and preservation of our furniture'. Wren's influence was seen in the increased height of rooms, with tall and well-proportioned sash windows. Fireplaces were surrounded with bolection mouldings in wood or stone, and walls of plaster or pine were divided into long panels with a carved frieze above. Some houses had door surrounds, picture frames and other parts decorated with the marvellously delicate and naturalistic carvings of Grinling Gibbons, the greatest of all English wood carvers, and his School. Mirrors now became tall and upright, with bevelled glass and arched headings often filled with mirror glass and finished with carved crestings. Some had distinctive glass borders in gilt mouldings or coloured glass banding; others had gesso frames. The interior of the house had a brightness which it had never seen before.

(4) Queen Anne
(1702–1714)

Queen Anne furniture is renowned for its simple dignity and good proportions. It shows how quickly and completely foreign techniques and

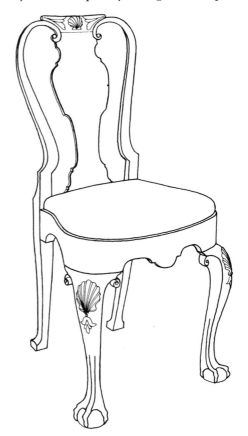

84 Carved walnut chair, early eighteenth century

34

85 Walnut chair, *c.* 1720, with cabriole
legs and claw-and-ball feet

86 Queen Anne period walnut stool with
cabriole legs

88 Early eighteenth-century
long-case clock, decorated
with arabesque ('seaweed')
marquetry

87 A Queen Anne walnut card table,
finely carved legs, claw-and-ball feet

styles had been first mastered, and then translated into a quiet English style. Rarely have sound craftsmanship, elegance and utility been so admirably blended.

The chairs of the period, with their emphasis on carefully-balanced curves, represent a distinct and novel development. They seem to have been influenced by chairs designed by Daniel Marot before 1700, with cabriole legs (curved supports adapted from animals' legs, in their earliest versions ending in hoofed feet) and wide pierced and elaborately carved splats enclosed by slightly curved uprights. These features were adapted and transformed by English craftsmen. At first chairs had vertical uprights with a curved cresting rail, a vase-shaped splat attached to the back seat by a moulded 'shoe', and narrow cabriole legs ending in clubbed feet and strengthened by turned stretchers. Later, the uprights took a more pronounced hoop form, the curve often relieved by a small angle at the hip, the bended splat was vase- or fiddle-shaped, and the cabriole legs became wider (84, 85). For the first time English chairs were made without stretchers, for the sturdy cabriole legs rendered these superfluous. The claw-and-ball foot, of oriental origin, representing a dragon's claw holding a jewel or ball, came into use on cabriole legs shortly after 1710, and was to have a long history, though the club foot persisted until 1750. On the best quality chairs the seat rails, which were rounded at the corners, and the splats and uprights, which were given a flat face for this purpose, were veneered with burr walnut and all four legs were of cabriole form, not, as was usual, only the front pair. Delicate carved ornament of shells and acanthus

90 Queen Anne desk and bookcase

leaves was found on the cresting rail, the knees of the legs, and the middle of the front seat rail. Chairs, stools (86) and settees were often made in sets. Upholstered settees were given short cabriole legs and lower backs, and one version of these (now known as 'love seats') was designed to seat two people. Settees also of chair-back form—two backs at first—were firmly established before the end of Anne's reign, and for the rest of the century were made in equal numbers with upholstered settees. In many houses it was customary for the women of the household to do their own upholstery in needlework with dyed wools on canvas—a cheap and hard-wearing material.

Mastery of good design was very evident in the case furniture of the period. Walnut of fine figure was almost invariably used for the best veneered pieces. Notable developments occurred in writing furniture. The bureau, in the form which is still familiar, that of a chest of drawers with a sloping flap, came into use soon after 1700 (89). Two sliders or lopers could be pulled out to support the flap for writing. With ample storage space provided by the drawers, this was a very practical piece. The older type of desk on stand, now on cabriole legs, continued in use, chiefly for ladies. Bureaux were also made in two stages, the

89 Queen Anne bureau

36

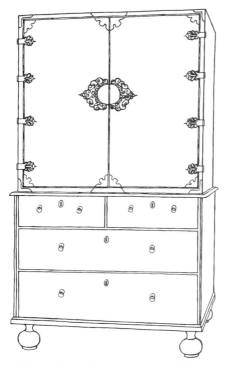

91 Queen Anne cabinet (Chinese style) on stand

92 Queen Anne tallboy with writing drawer

93 Queen Anne kneehole (pedestal)
dressing-table

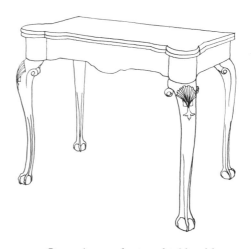

94 Queen Anne walnut card table with
cabriole legs and claw-and-ball feet

bureau-bookcase as we call it, but then known as the 'desk and bookcase' (77, 90). The lower stage was a fall-front bureau of the chest of drawers type, the upper a cabinet with glazed doors, arched domes or broken pediments, and finials. The bookcase section was often ingeniously fitted with small drawers, pigeon holes, etc. for filing papers. Small slides under the glass doors were for candlesticks. This fine piece of furniture became popular when the height of rooms increased.

Cabinets continued to be made in two types, those in the oriental style decorated with japan (91), and those designed for china and curiosities, veneered with walnut. Both types were found mounted on either a chest of drawers or on a stand with cabriole legs. Japanned cabinets were fashionable for most of the first half of the century, until the craze for japanning slowly died out. For curiosities the cabinet with small drawers remained popular, and some beautiful examples were produced. China cabinets closely resembled contemporary bookcases, and were very simple and finely proportioned. Their upper glazed sections, fitted with shelves, rested on cupboards with drawers.

Typical of the simple elegance of the time was the chest of drawers on bracket feet; the latter were far more satisfactory supports, from the point of view of design, than the former ball-and bun feet. For decoration the double half round moulding was now being employed on the rail between the drawers. A smaller version of chest of drawers (today called a 'bachelor's chest') had a folding top which could be supported on slides for writing. In some cases, however, chests of drawers were still mounted on cabriole-legged stands. When the latter were discarded, this type became the chest on chest, or tallboy, which was to remain popular during the century, in spite of the inconvenience of the top drawers. Sometimes the lower section had a writing flap (92).

One of the most attractive smaller pieces of the time was the dressing glass or toilet mirror, which came into fashion about 1700 and usually stood on a small dressing-table. These mirrors swung in uprights mounted on small stands with shaped fronts which had tiny drawers for the many toilet articles. In addition to the open type of dressing-table (now with cabriole legs), the knee-hole kind, of pedestal form, with drawers at each side of the central aperture, became very popular (93). Both kinds were seldom more than three feet wide, so that they could stand between the windows. The card table with square folding top and cabriole legs (one of which was movable to support the flap) appeared towards the end of Anne's reign (87, 94). The top had rounded corners for candlesticks and wells for the players' coins or counters. The mirrors which looked down on these tables now had a solid cresting, often with a shell decoration, a shaped base, and a narrower, flat frame round the glass itself (95).

95 Walnut mirror, early eighteenth century

The Georgian Period
(1714–1830)

◇

Early Georgian
(1714–1750)

General

THE Georgian era (1714–1830) has been rightly called the 'golden age' of English cabinet-making. The wealthy classes were enlightened patrons of the arts and crafts. Reared in an educational system which was firmly based on the study of Latin and Greek, they acquired a thorough knowledge of classical culture. This was rounded off by the grand tour of Europe, of three or four years' duration, which gave them a first-hand acquaintance with the finest craftsmanship of France and Italy. It also made them the world's greatest collectors of works of art, which they brought back to display in their homes. Land was a source of increasing wealth, expended on the building of great new houses. For merchants and bankers the way to social prestige and a political career lay in ownership of land. They therefore bought large estates and built houses like those of the landed aristocracy. No gentleman's attainments were complete without a sound knowledge of architecture, sculpture, painting, furniture, and interior decoration. It was the age of discerning amateurs—the dilettanti—who fostered good taste. 'Our nobility and gentry', wrote the Langley brothers in 1740, 'delight themselves now more than ever in the study of architecture, which enables them to distinguish good work and workmen from assuming pretenders.'

Encouraged by this patronage, furniture craftsmen reached a very high standard of skill. England's naval mastery enabled them to take their pick of the world's most beautiful timbers, among which mahogany became supreme. London was a magnet for provincial craftsmen of ability and ambition. Its style spread throughout England, partly through the country gentry who spent a season in the capital and ordered its furniture for their homes, and partly through the pattern books of furniture designs which were published for the benefit of rich patrons and craftsmen in the furniture industry.

(1) THE INTRODUCTION OF MAHOGANY

The accession of the Hanoverians in 1714 put the Whigs in power for nearly fifty years, as the Tories had discredited themselves by supporting the Stuarts. Led by Sir Robert Walpole (in office as virtually the first prime minister from 1721–42) the great Whig landowners (the 'Venetian oligarchy') aimed at peace and stability and the fostering of trade. Though war broke out with Spain in 1739, soon merging into a long struggle with France for colonial supremacy in North America and India, the administration had firmly established itself and confirmed national prosperity.

The style of the large country houses built at this time was dominated by the Palladian revival led by William Kent. The long gallery went out of fashion and was replaced by the sculpture gallery and library, which housed manuscripts and curiosities as well as books. Another innovation was the saloon, derived from the Italian *salone*, a large room which in Italy was used for dancing and gaming. The whole interior of the house was so arranged that the reception rooms, which were on the first floor, opened out of each other to provide views along the complete length of the floor. Mirrors were designed to catch the eye and reflect the scene from room to room.

Mahogany first began to affect the design of English furniture in the second quarter of the century. In 1721 Parliament abolished practically all the heavy duties on timbers grown in the British colonies in North America and the West Indies. The intention was to ensure plentiful supplies of timber for shipbuilding, but it naturally stimulated the trade in all kinds of timber for cabinet-making. Among the latter mahogany was the first to gain favour, and its import value rose from £43 in 1720 to nearly £30,000 in 1750. It was imported from the West Indies (including the Spanish colonies of San Domingo and Cuba, whence it was smuggled to Jamaica and then shipped to England to avoid the duty on foreign timber) and from Honduras in Central America.

It was a very strong wood, resistant to worm and free from warping, and it could be carved and pierced into delicate forms which were impossible in walnut. It had a beautiful patina, an attractive colouring, a range of fine figures, and large planks which were very suitable, for example, for table tops and doors. At first San Domingo wood was chiefly used. This was hard and heavy and lacked the figure of other varieties. Towards 1750 Cuban mahogany came into general use and had fine figures (including the famous 'Cuban curls') and rich colouring. Honduras mahogany (or 'baywood' from the Bay of Honduras) was in use mainly after 1750. It was lighter in weight and colour than the other two.

When mahogany was first introduced there were increased imports of dark Virginia walnut. Both woods were largely unfigured, and this encouraged the construction of furniture in the solid, with carved decoration. Virginia walnut was often stained to represent mahogany. But mahogany took some time to have any far-reaching influence on furniture styles, its earliest impact being to promote bolder and more elaborate carving. Until 1750 probably as much furniture was still made in walnut as in mahogany, but much of the walnut furniture of this period has disappeared owing to its perishable nature.

For a long time chairs continued to be made with cabriole legs ending with claw-and-ball, lion's paw or pad feet. After about 1725 chair knees had vigorously carved lion and satyr masks, shells, and cabochons (ornamental polished jewels in decorative borders)(105), the arms often ended in eagles' heads, the solid splats now became more open with vertical piercing, and top rails were flatter (96).

Chests of drawers retained their traditional shape with bracket or small cabriole feet. Mouldings, however, were transferred from the carcase to the edges of drawers, at first in the form of lip mouldings (from about 1710), then, after about 1730, cock beads, which from 1745 until the end of the century became the predominant decoration of this kind. Another form of chest of drawers, the commode, arrived from France in George II's reign. It was an ornamental piece designed for the drawing room and at first had carved friezes, feet, corners and drawer fronts. Tallboys kept to plainer form; the frieze had a cavetto moulding until about 1735, then became flat.

When mahogany, with its wider planks,

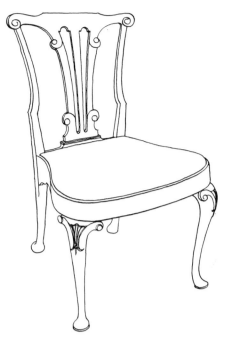

96 George I walnut chair

gradually came into more general use, extending dining-tables, with a separate leaf which could be inserted in the centre when required, made their appearance. But dining-tables with gate-legs and oval or circular tops, of the kind which had been made since Charles II's reign, and now with four or six cabriole legs, remained very strongly in favour. About 1750 a convenient form in three units was common—a central gate-leg with rectangular flaps, and two semicircular side tables which could be placed at each end.

An ingenious extending (or 'concertina') frame was given to square card tables so that two legs could swing out to support the flap, thus avoiding the somewhat ungainly appearance of the opened table when only one movable leg was used. About 1730, when mahogany card tables were being made, square projecting corners replaced the former rounded ones, and this form was to remain popular for some thirty years. Another innovation was the tea table. Tea-drinking had been spreading rapidly since 1660 and had at first taken place in public tea-gardens. These became too crowded for the well-to-do who after about 1725 gradually took to drinking tea in their own homes. The small tripod table, with a round top supported on a central pillar and three feet of cabriole form ('pillar and claw') was so serviceable for this purpose that it was in general use by 1750 (97). The top, which was made

40

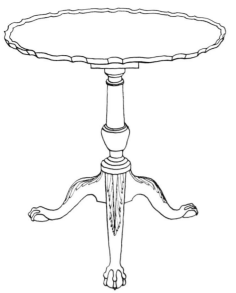

97 Mid eighteenth-century tripod ('pillar-and-claw') table

to tilt so that the table could stand against the wall when not in use, had a scalloped and raised edge, or a little gallery (117), to save the fragile and expensive tea things from being swept off. There were also rectangular tea tables with cabriole legs (110).

The libraries of large houses had pedestal library tables which stood in the middle of the room and so were decorated with a great deal of carving, though they avoided the excessive richness of decoration of the French models from which they were copied. These tables had drawers and cupboards in the pedestals; the centre was left open or had a recessed cupboard.

A feature of this period was the architectural character of larger case furniture and of mirrors. Bookcases and cabinets, for instance, lost the simple appearance they had in Anne's reign and now acquired broken pediments, classical cornices, capitals and pilasters. About 1745 the large 'breakfront' library bookcases with a centre section flanked by two slightly recessed wings was introduced. The bureau-bookcase had already had some architectural features, and these, e.g. broken or swan-neck pediments, and pilasters framing the upper mirror or panel were retained until the mid-century. Mirrors had the same kinds of pediments, enclosing shells, cartouches or plinths, and curved or straight bases (98). Gesso or walnut or mahogany veneers with gilt mouldings were often used. Long-case clocks were now taller, and were decorated with figured walnut or japan and crowned with arched hoods, domes and finials. Much gilt gesso furniture was also made until about 1730 (102, 103).

(2) WILLIAM KENT AND BAROQUE FURNITURE

William Kent (1685–1748) occupies a special place in the history of English furniture for he was the first English architect to design furniture as an essential part of his interior decoration. Of humble birth, he showed early promise as an artist, and it was as a student in Rome that he met the Earl of Burlington who recognised his abilities, became his patron and introduced him at Court. From 1720 he showed such amazing versatility in the whole field of architecture and the decorative arts—even in landscape gardening and dress designing—that he became the arbiter of fashionable taste until his death. Burlington was the leading advocate of the Palladian revival and it was in this style that Kent designed Chiswick House for his patron, and Holkham for the Earl of Leicester. For his interiors, however, both in these houses and in the royal palaces and other buildings where he worked, Kent favoured the rich baroque style of furniture which he had seen in Venice and which was designed to impress with its boldness and grandeur. His furniture, therefore,

98 George I or II gilt gesso mirror

41

was on a magnificent scale which may appear extravagant ('often immeasurably ponderous'—Horace Walpole) though it was perfectly in keeping with the setting for which it was designed. It did, however, have a monumental character more suitable for stone than wood, and it showed the limitations of furniture designed by an architect and not by a craftsman.

Kent made great play with elaborately carved festoons, shells, masks, acanthus leaves, cherubs, human figures, and lion heads and paws, and with decorative ornaments like the Greek key pattern (99) and the Vitruvian scroll (101, 104).

101 Console table carved and gilt with marble top, *c.* 1730

99 Greek key pattern (from the *Works in Architecture*) 1773–1822

Much of his furniture was richly gilded, sometimes of mahogany partly- (or 'parcel-') gilt. Typical of his style were his large side tables (100),

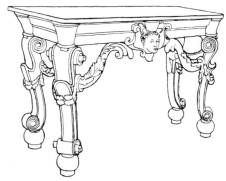

100 Carved and gilt side table in the William Kent style with marble top

five or six feet long, supported on scroll legs, figures, sphinxes or animals, linked by swags of foliage, flowers or fruit, and surmounted by tops of Italian marble (hence their name of 'marble tables') or of mosaic, gesso or scagliola (an artificial compound with a high polish). Closely related to the side tables were the smaller console (or 'clap') tables introduced from France shortly after 1700. Their supports often took the form of an eagle with outstretched wings (101, 104), or of a pair of dolphins. Above these tables were large pier-glasses of distinct architectural character enriched by mouldings which matched those on doorways, cornices and window architraves.

Kent's furniture was designed for a few great houses, but it seems to have inspired the architec-

tural spirit of much of the furniture made for smaller houses after 1725. Its influence was also evident in some of the furniture plates in Batty and Thomas Langley's *Treasury of Designs* of 1740, a pattern book intended chiefly for the building trade but including a few furniture designs.

Thomas Chippendale and the Mid-Century Styles
(1750–1765)

Chippendale has become a household name in England as that of the most famous of all English cabinet-makers. His commanding position, however, has been somewhat modified as the result of recent research, and his reputation now rests more on his skill as a designer and interpreter than as a craftsman. He was born at Otley, Yorkshire, in 1718, migrated to London as a young man, set up shop in Conduit Court, Long Acre, and then, from 1753 until his death in 1779, had large premises in St Martin's Lane, the chief cabinet-making centre of London. He had rich and influential clients but never became a royal cabinet-maker. In this respect he was surpassed by two outstanding craftsmen, William Vile and John Cobb, who were business partners and his neighbours, and held royal appointments between them for almost twenty years.

Chippendale's fame is securely based on his pattern book, *A Gentleman and Cabinet-Maker's Director*, (160 plates) of 1754. Books with some furniture designs (e.g. by the Langley brothers in 1740) had already appeared in England, but they were written by builders, architects and artists,

102

102 Early eighteenth-century gilt gesso chair

103 Early eighteenth-century gilt gesso side table

103

104

104 Console table of the William Kent
period

105 Mahogany armchair *c.* 1750; carved
detail includes cabochon on knee

105

and their furniture plates were subordinate to other decoration and were of no particular merit. Chippendale's book, on the other hand, was the first to be devoted entirely to furniture and the first to be produced by a practising cabinet-maker. It was an immediate success and the fore-runner of numerous similar books by craftsmen. It had a second edition in 1755 and a third (revised and enlarged) in 1762. There has been a long controversy as to whether Chippendale him-self did the drawings for the plates (which all bear his signature) or employed two designers, M. Lock and H. Copland, to do them for him, but there now seems little doubt that he was personally responsible for them. The designs presented the prevailing furniture fashions and were executed (often in a modified form) by cabinet-makers throughout the country. The few surviving pieces that can be definitely identified as made in Chippendale's workshop from his own designs (it is unlikely that he would have had time to make any himself) are undoubtedly of high, but not exceptional, quality. In fact, his best work was done, not in his own *Director* styles, but later, in the quite different style of Robert Adam. Thus 'Chippendale' is not a maker's label but a very convenient term for the furniture in the original designs of the mid-century.

The *Director* designs had three elements. The

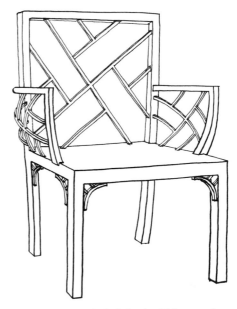

107 Beechwood chair in the Chinese style, *c.* 1760–5

chief was the Rococo, the others were the Chinese and the Gothic. To a great extent they were blended together and remained fashionable until about 1765. The Rococo (*rocaille*) came to England from France where it had originated about 1700. It was a reaction against the massive and monu-mental Baroque, and was characterised by delicate scroll work, asymmetrical in form and executed in intricate C and S curves (106, 119). Interest in this French style was evident in England soon after 1740, and several small pattern books incorporated the new decoration for the use of carvers and artists. Lock and Copland were pioneers in this work, and included in their books a few furniture designs (e.g. mirrors, console tables and picture frames). Chippendale applied the rococo style to all kinds of furniture but care-fully modified it (in spite of a few exaggerated designs) to suit English traditions and avoid the excessive decoration which prevailed in France. It is this English Rococo (described in the *Director* as the 'modern taste') which explains the typical curves on so much of the furniture of the period.

Chippendale took full advantage of the revived interest in Chinese decoration ('chinoiserie'), which was largely stimulated by the translation from the French in 1741 of du Halde's travel book on the Chinese empire, to design furniture in a style sometimes called 'Chippendale Chinese'. Already a number of pattern books of Chinese

106 'Ribband-back' carved mahogany chair

designs (notably by M. Darly) had been published in England, and some large houses had a Chinese room with imported hand-painted Chinese wallpaper and suitably designed Chinese furniture. The Chinese style had two main features: one was geometrical lattice (107) or fret work (114), the other scrollwork mingled with Eastern motives such as dragons, long-necked birds, icicles, bulrushes, pagodas, bells and tiny mandarins.

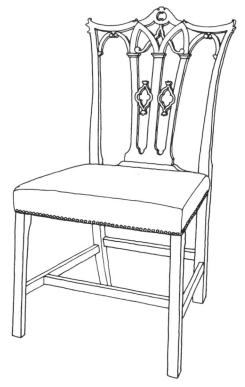

108 Carved mahogany 'Gothic' chair, *c.* 1760–5

The mid-century Gothic, unlike the other two *Director* styles, was English in origin and owed its special features to Horace Walpole, whose letters give us such a vivid picture of the social life of the time. Walpole was not a complete innovator for there was still a living tradition of Gothic crafts linked to their mediaeval origins. What he did was to make a highly personal contribution to Gothic decoration. In 1750 he began to turn his house at Strawberry Hill, Twickenham, into a Gothic villa, decorating the interior with delicate Gothic tracery copied from outstanding examples of English and foreign mediaeval work. This tracery, again, blended happily with rococo decoration (108). Walpole's Gothic was imitated by his admirers, and the *Director* caught the

fashion by including designs of furniture with pinnacles, arcading and pointed arches, in fret work or carving.

The emphasis was now on delicate and fanciful decoration in intricate curves. William Hogarth, the famous artist, wrote in his *Analysis of Beauty* (1753) that 'the waving line is more productive of beauty than any of the former (i.e. circular and straight lines) for which reason we shall call it the line of beauty. The serpentine line hath the power of super-adding grace to beauty'.

Chippendale's graceful and versatile designs were particularly evident in his chairs. The great strength of mahogany led to delicate and pierced work on chair backs which would have been much too daring in other woods. Rococo chairs had open splats carved with varieties of C and S scrolls under a cresting rail of serpentine ('cupid's bow') shape (116), the more ornate versions being the famous 'ribband backs' (106) which closely followed French models. The cabriole leg was still used but the claw-and-ball foot was being replaced by delicate French scroll toe. Some chairs had straight legs and stretchers. The re-introduction of the stretcher, after being out of fashion for fifty years, raises an interesting point of design, for structurally, and especially in mahogany, it was quite unnecessary. Chinese chairs (107) had lattice work in the backs and between the arms and seat, and fret-cut brackets in the angles between legs and seat; the legs were usually square in section and had carved or pierced frets. Some chairs made in this style at the time were of beech. On Gothic chairs (108) pointed arches were found in the splat, or filled the whole space between the uprights.

Commodes in the French taste (109) were now so fashionable that all decorative pieces with drawers were called 'commodes', and the term chest of drawers dropped temporarily out of use. Rococo carving, serpentine fronts, gadrooned

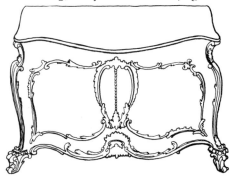

109 'Commode table' (from the *Director* 1762)

edges and bright, ornate gilt handles were all indications of this French influence. Some commodes, intended for Chinese bedrooms, were japanned.

As a general rule, tables in the rococo style had cabriole legs, those in the Gothic and Chinese styles straight legs, Chinese tables having fret work on the legs and frieze. The massive side tables of the baroque period gradually passed out of fashion, but tables of this kind, while of smaller proportions and more restrained decoration, still had marble tops. Console tables, in contrast, retained much of their ornate character, sometimes with extravagant asymmetrical decoration.

110 Chippendale period tea table

The *Director* indeed had some intricate designs for these tables which, perhaps fortunately, do not seem to have been executed at all. The fashionable mahogany china (or tea) table with a gallery (110) was illustrated in the *Director*, with suggested designs for the Chinese fret to decorate the gallery.

Library tables (111) were predominantly of the open pedestal type for which there was evidently a considerable demand, as the number of their designs went up from six in the first edition of the *Director* to eleven in the third. Bookcases were also creating much interest, for the 1762 edition had fourteen designs for them. The breakfront type was popular (112, 118), of good proportions and architectural features, and with graceful mahogany glazing bars of lattice form. Desks and bookcases (113) had glazed doors panelled in thin mouldings, sometimes in smaller geometrical panes divided by fanciful tracery. Some bookcases and 'desks and bookcases' had pierced pediments and fretted galleries. Chippendale also had a number of designs for cabinets (114) of various kinds to display curiosities or china, some

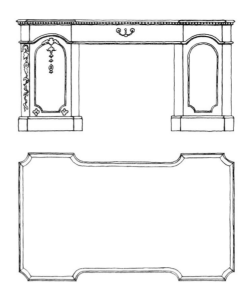

111 Library table (from the *Director* 1762)

of the china cabinets being small ones for hanging on the wall. The pole (or fire) screen on a tripod base, with movable screen to ward off the heat of the fire, was another popular piece (115).

Perhaps the best examples of the free expression of rococo asymmetry, often combined with Chinese decoration, and providing a distinct contrast to former architectural forms, were the carved and gilt frames of large mirrors (119), on which the most intricate arrangement of scrolls and foliage might be mingled with chinoiserie.

For about two decades after 1740 long-case clocks were not so fashionable as the smaller mahogany bracket clocks, and the cartel clocks,

112 Library bookcase (from the *Director* 1762)

origining in France, which had ornate carved and gilt arms and were made to hang on the wall.

It was William Vile who at this period produced some outstanding masterpieces of English craftsmanship. Among them, all made for Queen Charlotte, were, in 1761, a bureau-cabinet with superb rococo carving on the base and delicate Chinese fret work enclosing the upper stage, and a jewel cabinet on stand with carving, ivory inlays and veneers all of the highest quality; and, in 1762, a magnificent mahogany bookcase decorated with what is probably the finest carving ever seen on a piece of English furniture.

114 Chippendale period china case

113 Desk and bookcase (from the *Director* 1762)

115 Chippendale period tripod pole (or fire) screen.

48

Chippendale

116 Mahogany chair with back very similar to design in Chippendale's *Director*

117 Mahogany tripod table, *c.* 1765, with fretted gallery

118 Mahogany breakfront bookcase of the Chippendale period

119 Painted pine rococo mirror frame probably by Thomas Johnson, *c.* 1755

Robert Adam (1728–1792) and the Neo-Classical Style

Shortly after the third edition of the *Director* (1762) the Rococo was in decline (though chinoiseries and the Gothic continued in some favour) owing to the creation of a new style by Robert Adam, the second and most important of four Scottish brothers who set up as architects in London. Like Kent, Adam had wealthy patrons, and designed houses and their interiors as single entities (e.g. Harewood, Nostell, Kenwood, Syon, Osterley), but he went further than Kent in designing every part of the interior down to the smallest detail, including lighting, carpets, clocks, and metal fittings of fireplaces and doors, to an extent unknown before.

Adam's style marked a return to classical forms. As a young man he had thoroughly mastered classical principles through his travels in Italy and his excavations of the ruins of Diocletian's palace at Spalato (modern Split) in Dalmatia. He was also strongly influenced by the decorative work of Raphael and his pupils in Rome, itself based on the stucco decoration of the ancient Romans, and of the early Christians in the catacombs (their grotto decorations giving us the word 'grotesques'). He himself described grotesques as 'that beautiful light style of ornament used by the ancient Romans, by far the most perfect that has ever appeared for inside decorations'.

But Adam was no mere imitator. From these varied sources he produced his own delicate and graceful versions of the classical style, the neo-classical, which caused a revolution in decoration and furnishing. He employed his own group of foreign artists and plasterers to decorate walls and ceilings, mostly with a background of pastel shades. Furniture was made to his design by several firms, including Chippendale's. Typical of Adam's motives for furniture were swags of husks (127), rams' heads, the honeysuckle (120), urns, paterae and medallions. These were carved in low relief, inlaid, painted or mounted in ormolu. Adam's fine inlay work was the same in

technique as the marquetry of the walnut period, but differed from it in its more delicate colouring and its emphasis on classical forms. Ormolu mounts, of brightly gilded bronze and brass which made an excellent show on a dark mahogany ground, were formerly imported from France, but after 1762 were made at the Soho Works, Birmingham, by Matthew Boulton, partner of the great engineer, James Watt. As well as reviving marquetry Adam made much use of satinwood, of light yellow colour, and attractive figure which came up well under polish; it was imported from the West and East Indies and mainly used as a veneer.

Adam's furniture was designed for particular rooms to his clients' orders. His chairs, lighter than those of the Chippendale era, had backs of both curved (especially oval) (121) and rectilinear (including the 'lyre-back') form (122). He favoured tapered legs ending on small plinths. As rich people were still attracted by French fashions, many upholstered chairs at this time closely followed French models and were covered with expensive materials. Some of them had the final versions of cabriole legs, of graceful serpentine shape on scroll feet.

Particularly linked with Adam's name is the

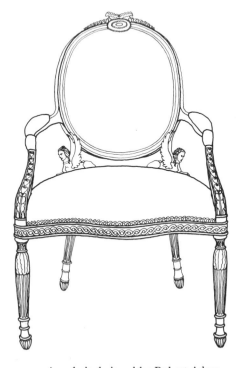

121 Armchair designed by Robert Adam for Osterley, *c.* 1777

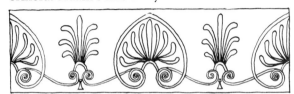

120 Honeysuckle or anthemion (from the *Works in Architecture* 1773–1822)

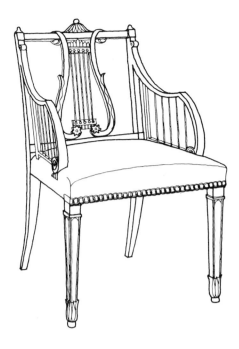

124 Adam pedestal and urn: one of two flanking dining table (from the *Works in Architecture* 1773–1822)

122 Adam-style 'lyre-back' chair, *c.* 1775

sideboard-table, forerunner of the modern sideboard. This was a composite piece: a side table, with a detached pedestal cupboard supporting an urn at each side, and a wine cooler underneath (123, 124). The pedestals were used as

123 Adam dining-room sideboard table (from the *Works in Architecture* 1773–1822)

plate warmers or cellarets, the urns as knife cases or containers for water. Tapered legs without stretchers gave long mahogany tables attractive proportions (125). Adam also designed smaller semicircular side tables, often gilded. It was at this time that the Pembroke table (133, 139), with two (usually semicircular) flaps, came into fashion. Some of these smaller tables had the final version of the cabriole leg (131).

Some very fine commodes were made in this

period inlaid with classical motives and figures (132). Outstanding among them was one supplied by Chippendale to Harewood House in 1773, almost certainly to Adam's design, and known as the 'Diana and Minerva' commode from its

125 Adam style side table

inlaid figures. It cost £86, the largest sum known to have been charged by Chippendale for a piece of case furniture. Only large mirrors cost more, owing to the expense of the glass. Adam's designs for commodes also included one of semicircular shape for the Countess of Derby (126, 127).

Adam's mirrors, carefully designed to conform to his decorative schemes, were of graceful proportions, the larger ones usually having rectangular (128) carved and gilt frames, the smaller ones both oval (129) and rectangular frames.

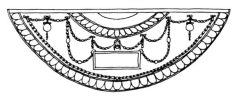

126 Adam commode in the Countess of
Derby's dressing-room (from the *Works in
Architecture* 1773-1822)

127 Top of the commode

129 Adam pier glass (from the *Works in
Architecture* 1773–1882)

128 Adam pier glass (from the *Works in
Architecture* 1773–1822)

130 Carved mahogany 'ladder back'
chair showing last phase of the cabriole
leg, *c.* 1775

Adam and Hepplewhite

131

131 Adam style mahogany card table

132 Small commode of the Hepplewhite period in the French taste decorated with marquetry

133 Mahogany Pembroke table inlaid with boxwood and stained sycamore *c.* 1785

134 Mahogany quartetto tables *c.* 1785

133

132

134

George Hepplewhite (*d.* 1786) and the *Guide*

Hepplewhite's name must always be coupled with Adam's, for he successfully adapted the neoclassical style to all types of furniture for the general public. He was not a prominent craftsman, and little is known of his life beyond the facts that he had been an apprentice to Gillow of Lancaster, migrated to London, and had a shop in Cripplegate. So far, no single piece of furniture has been identified as his work. His fame now rests on his pattern book, the *Cabinet-Maker and Upholsterer's Guide*, which he did not even live to see published, for it came out in 1788, two years after his death, and was issued by A. Hepplewhite and Co. (his widow, Alice, being then in charge of the firm). It is uncertain how far Hepplewhite was personally responsible for the designs (nearly 300 in number) of the *Guide*, but it was the most important pattern book that had appeared for

over twenty years, and was an immediate success, for a second edition was published in 1789, and a third, revised, in 1794. It did not claim originality; its intention, in the words of its short preface, was 'to unite elegance and utility', to be 'useful to the mechanic and serviceable to the gentleman', and to 'convey a just idea of English taste in furniture'. It illustrated, in its popularisation of Adam's work, simple, light and graceful furniture, avoiding exaggeration and showing a masterly feeling for ornament. It represented the style generally adopted by cabinet-makers in the last quarter of the eighteenth century.

Hepplewhite is associated with oval and particularly shield-back (135) chairs, but he did not invent either kind. He was, however, possibly responsible for introducing the Prince of Wales's feathers (136) as a chair decoration. Among other

136 Chair back with three feathers (from the *Guide* 1794)

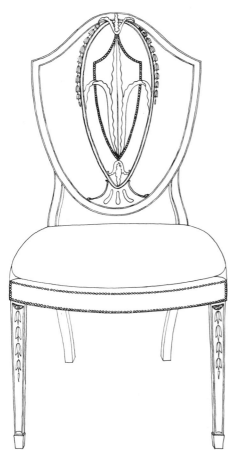

135 Shield back chair (from the *Guide* 1794)

carved, inlaid or painted motives which were recommended for the fillings of chair backs were wheat-ears, urns, draperies, rosettes and swags of husks. Square-back chairs (136) were also illustrated in the *Guide*, and a larger selection of these appeared in the 1794 edition, probably to compete with Sheraton, who in his *Drawing-Book* of 1791–4 criticised Hepplewhite's designs, and especially those of his chairs, as having 'already caught the decline'.

A feature of most of these backs was that the bottom of the shield, or the bottom rail of square-backs, did not directly join the seat. Chair legs were of round or square section, and usually

137 Sideboard (from the *Guide* 1794)

139 Pembroke table (from the *Guide* 1794)

straight and tapered, those of square section often ending on spade feet (135). Some feet, however, turned outwards. Mahogany, with carved decoration, was generally the material for chairs; the seat upholstery, plain or striped, normally covered the seat rails, secured by brass-headed nails. Japanned or painted chairs, matching the colour scheme of the room, were of lighter construction and had cane seats, covered with cushions. The *Guide* had several designs for stools, in mahogany or japan, *en suite* with the chairs.

Two kinds of sideboard were illustrated in the *Guide*. The more formal kind followed Adam's arrangement of side table and flanking pedestals with urns, one of the pedestals being lined with tin to take a heater and serve as a plate warmer. The other kind was a useful compact piece with canted side cupboards incorporated within the table, and a central long drawer of bow or serpentine form (137). The side cupboards had partitions, one of which was lined with lead to hold water. It was a well-established custom to

wash dirty glasses in the dining-room during a meal.

Dainty and elegant small tables were a feature of Hepplewhite's designs. Their recommended height was not to exceed 28 in., except that of the more ornamental pier tables. The tops of the latter, and of the finer Pembroke and card tables (138), were often elaborately inlaid or painted. The Pembroke tables (133, 139) had two flaps, oval or rectangular. Table legs were of graceful tapered form, square or round in section. Round and kidney-shaped tables were also now in use. Library tables were generally of mahogany, 3 to 4 ft long and 3 ft deep, with a recessed centre and flanking cupboards, each surmounted by a drawer.

Hepplewhite chests of drawers were of particularly graceful proportions. They were often bow or serpentine (140) fronted and had outward curving feet, between which was an apron piece

138 Top of card table (from the *Guide* 1794)

140 Chest of drawers (from the *Guide* 1794)

141 Secretaire-bookcase (from the *Guide* 1794)

143 Wardrobe (from the *Guide* 1794)

of curved outline. Tallboys kept more closely to their traditional form, but were now becoming out-of-date. Outward curving feet were also found on some bureau-bookcases, as were, at times, delicately scrolled, openwork pediments. The types known as 'secretaire-bookcases' had, instead of a sloping front, a top drawer which let down to form the writing surface (141).

The *Guide* illustrated the semicircular commode (142) for the drawing-room, a shape which by 1780 had become very fashionable, though

destined to have a comparatively short life. This type usually had a single large door in front, and for its decoration satinwood panels, painted or inlaid, were recommended. Another popular piece was the clothes press or wardrobe (143)

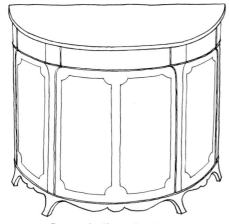

142 Commode (from the *Guide* 1794)

144 Bed (from the *Guide* 1794)

which had, enclosed by solid doors, an upper stage with shelves (as clothes were then laid flat and not hung up) and a lower stage of two long and two short drawers. Among the larger pieces of the period were breakfront library bookcases, the lower part containing drawers and cupboard, and the upper part shelves enclosed by glazed doors, with glazing bars in a wide variety of graceful patterns.

Pier glasses, according to Hepplewhite, were to be designed so as to fill almost all the pier and to be 'good carved work, gilt and burnished'. Rectangular shapes were fashionable and were given openwork cresting pieces and bases. By this time bedposts were exposed and of graceful proportions. Their cornices were much simplified and often matched those above windows (144).

Thomas Sheraton (1751–1806) and the *Drawing-Book*

Sheraton, the last of the famous trio of Georgian designers, was an obscure journeyman cabinet-maker from Stockton-on-Tees who came to London about 1790. There is no evidence that he ever had a workshop there of his own, or made and sold furniture. He probably developed his designs by picking up ideas from what he saw in cabinet-makers' shops. He eked out a poor living as a writer and teacher of drawing in Wardour Street, where he died in poverty. His most important work, *The Cabinet-Maker's and Up-holsterer's Drawing-Book*, appeared in parts between 1791–4. Its 113 plates, of excellent draughtsmanship, and with fuller technical notes than any other similar work, illustrated the final version of the neo-classical style, and revealed great originality and versatility. The book had some 600 subscribers from the trade in all parts of the country and undoubtedly had considerable influence. 'Sheraton', in fact, is a well-earned label for some of the most elegant and technically perfect furniture ever made in England. His later *Cabinet Dictionary* (1803) lacked the sure touch of the *Drawing-Book*, though it contained the first published designs of the new Regency style, while his unfinished *Encyclopaedia* (1804–8), compiled when his mind was apparently unsound, borders on the fantastic.

A distinguishing feature of this period was the production of much well-proportioned, portable, compact and multi-purpose furniture which often incorporated ingenious mechanical devices. After 1760 interest in mechanisation was everywhere prevalent, stimulated by the inventions in the cotton and other industries and by the general quickening of industrial activity which heralded the 'Industrial Revolution'. There was a big increase towards the end of the century in the number of patents for furniture and upholstery registered at the Patent Office. Social conditions in London created a demand for this kind of furniture, for the pressure of population, and the lack of transport facilities which kept most people close to their places of work, made living conditions more cramped, even among the middle classes. Many of Sheraton's pieces were intended to be easily movable, either about a room, or from room to room. Portability had returned to furniture.

Sheraton recommended that his designs should be executed mainly in satinwood, mahogany and rosewood, or in painted wood, especially in white and gold. His decoration at first included cross-banding, carving, inlay and painting. The publication of the *Drawing-Book*, however, coincided with the outbreak of the long war with France which merged into the life and death struggle with Napoleon (1793–1815). The resultant rise in the cost of living imposed a need for economy, and expensive methods of decoration like carving and fine inlay were gradually replaced by cheaper processes, such as painting and stringing (i.e. inlay in fine lines of wood or brass to contrast with the surrounding veneer) (146).

Sheraton differed from Hepplewhite in emphasising square and rectangular elevations, particularly in chairs, sofas and mirrors, though in plan his furniture often had curved and serpentine outlines. In direct contrast to Hogarth's waving line of beauty, the fashion now was for straight lines. 'The greatest delicacy which can be given to the Form', wrote A. Alison in 1790 (*Essays on the Nature and Principles of Taste*), 'is rather in the use of direct and angular lines, than in waving and serpentine ones.'

The chair designs in the *Drawing-Book* had backs of predominantly rectangular shape (149) (there were only two examples of shield backs) with vertical fillings and usually straight and narrow top and bottom rails, the latter being normally clear of the seat. Parlour chairs had straight-fronted seats, drawing-room chairs shaped or round seats. Tapered legs, mostly of cylindrical form, and decorated with reeding, were favoured. The arms often swept up in a pronounced S-curve

145 Two small basin stands of the Sheraton period

148 Windsor chair in yew in Gothic style, c. 1750

147 Small side table of Sheraton period with tea caddy

146 Davenport writing cabinet rosewood inlaid with stringing
lines of brass, c. 1805

from extensions of the front legs to join the uprights near the top rail. Cheaper chairs of beech, japanned and gilt, with cane seats, were also made in large quantities at this time.

Cylinder desks, with a tambour front (i.e. a roll front of narrow strips of wood on a canvas backing) were now popular. Some had bookcases (150) with graceful glazing bars, surmounted by curved or swan-neck pediments, or by straight cornices. As an alternative to the cylinder front was the older type of deep top drawer falling as a quadrant.

Pier tables, of light and elegant form, were usually of satinwood, though some had marble tops. Their legs were round in section and had stretchers, intended to make 'the under part appear more finished' (151). For card tables, Sheraton advocated square tapered legs decorated with stringing or inlaid panels. The *Drawing-Book* showed two varieties of oval library tables, for which mahogany, carved or inlaid was considered

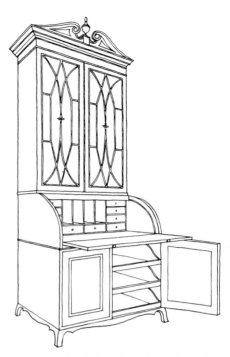

150 Cylinder desk and bookcase (from the *Drawing-Book* 1791–4)

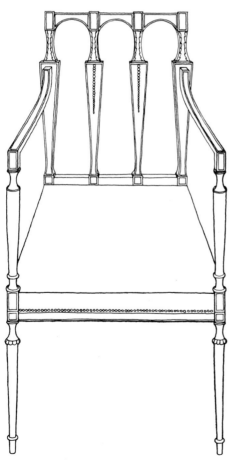

149 Chair design (from the *Drawing-Book* 1791–4)

most suitable. In one example it was stated that 'brass mouldings could be used to advantage'—a forecast of the brass decoration of the Regency. A 'kidney table' for the library—a shape borrowed from France and also used for a design for a lady's work table—was less successful, the round pedestal ends not being really a practical shape for the drawers. A very popular new type of table for writing came in after 1790; this was the Carlton House table (though it had apparently no connection with that place, the Prince of Wales's London residence), of rectangular shape and with a small gallery of drawers and cupboards on the top at the sides and back. One of the most attractive features of the *Drawing-Book* was its varied designs for dwarf writing, reading, work and dressing tables, largely for ladies' use (152). Many occasional and tea tables used the well-established pillar and claw support, and a particularly graceful version of the claw, concave in form, ending on a peg foot, was widely used after 1790. This tripod base also continued on candle stands and pole screens (or fire screens) (115), but the cheval ('horse') fire screens had wider panels set between two uprights (153). The same kind of framework with a rectangular mirror was known as a cheval glass.

151 Pier table (from the *Drawing-Book* 1791–4)

Sideboards were similar to those of the Hepplewhite period, except that they often had brass galleries for the display of plate. The *Drawing-Book* had one design for the combined table and flanking pedestal cupboards. Chests of drawers ('dressing chests') remained simple in form; the top drawer was sometimes fitted for writing, but by 1800 it became usual to have a deep frieze below the top.

153 Horse fire screen (from the *Drawing-Book* 1791–4)

The ingeniously fitted furniture of the time often required quite complicated internal mechanism. A 'Harlequin' Pembroke table (154), for instance, in the *Drawing-Book*, was a combined writing and breakfast table; a small nest of drawers rose from within the table top as soon as the fly bracket supporting one of the flaps was turned, yet a turn of a key rendered this mechanism inoperative, and both flaps could be set up to give a flat surface. A library table incorporating an adjustable framework with a set of library steps, and a lady's dressing commode which

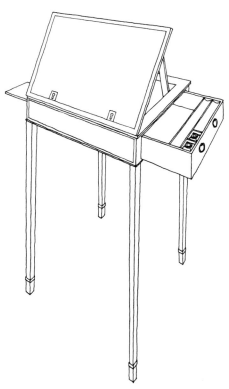

152 Reading and working table (from the *Drawing-Book* 1791–4)

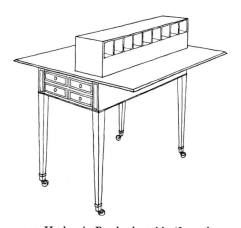

154 Harlequin Pembroke table (from the *Drawing-Book* 1791–4)

included a wash stand and writing desk, are further examples of Sheraton's compact pieces.

Some of Sheraton's designs may be criticised as carrying delicacy of appearance to the point of fragility, sometimes, perhaps, at the expense of comfort, usefulness and strength. Occasionally, too, ingenuity may have been misplaced. His use of draperies on some pieces was highly fanciful; as in his designs for beds, while the deep festooned and fringed covering round the top of two ladies' work tables forecast the Victorian habit of hiding the structural framework of furniture beneath upholstered padding. But beyond all doubt his furniture generally had a purity of line and attractiveness of form, without loss of utility, which have never been surpassed. He fully deserves his posthumous fame as one of the most original of English furniture designers.

The Regency Period

1800–1830

'REGENCY' is the name given to a revived classical style which was in vogue between 1800 and 1830 (and which thus overlapped the political Regency of 1811–20 from which it takes its name). It was a reaction against Adam's neo-classicism in that it sought to reproduce or adapt closely actual pieces of ancient furniture. At first this new approach, already evident in some of Sheraton's designs, was made with care and understanding, but it later became an antiquarian pursuit with a strong archaeological bias, and ended in much incongruous copying of antique pieces and ornament. Thus although Regency furniture could still show good proportions and workmanship it was also beginning to lack originality in design. The style was related to (but was not a close version of) the classical revival in France under the Directoire (1795–9) and Empire (1804–14) which, owing to Napoleon's conquests and to the publication in 1812 of the work of its two outstanding designers, C. Percier and P. Fontaine, gradually spread over much of Europe. The Regency style was formerly known as 'English Empire'.

In England the earliest source of inspiration was the Greek revival, which had begun before 1800 and which was to have a long life, 'the travels of scientific men—the publications within the last twenty years—the Elgin marbles, all alike detailing the perfection of Grecian architecture and ornament' (G. Smith, 1826). The pioneer of the Regency was Henry Holland (1745–1806), the gifted architect, whose furniture designs, beginning in the Adam style, later used effective Greek detail (e.g. at Woburn, Carlton House and Southill) in a restrained and elegant classicism. Throughout the Regency period (and indeed much later) 'Grecian' became a popular term among cabinet-makers. Holland was followed by Thomas Hope (1768–1831), a rich scholar, traveller and collector, who in 1807 published a book of drawings, *Household Furniture and Interior Decoration* (2, 156, 166). This illustrated his designs for the furniture made for his house at Deepdene, Surrey, where he had a magnificent collection of antiquities. In order, as he wrote, to associate 'all the elegances of antique forms with all the requirements of modern customs and habits', he both imitated antique furniture and designed pieces of his own day, unknown in ancient times, to accord with his theories. He drew inspiration from all parts of the ancient world—Greece, Rome and Egypt. Interest in Egypt had been stimulated by Napoleon's Egyptian campaign and Nelson's brilliant victory at the Nile (1798), and by the publication in 1802 of a survey of Egypt by the French scholar, V. Denon, who had accompanied Napoleon.

The designers who followed Hope lacked his knowledge and strict interpretation of antiquity. The chief was the cabinet-maker George Smith, whose *Collection of Designs for Household Furniture and Interior Decoration* (1808), with 158 plates 'studied from the best antique examples', popularised the new style, and showed traces of extravagance and search for novelty. Smith also published *The Cabinet-Maker's and Upholsterer's Guide* in 1826, in which he admitted that his designs of 1808 were now largely obsolete.

155 Lotus bud

The chief features of Regency furniture were simplicity of outline, and straight, unbroken surfaces emphasising horizontal and vertical lines. Greco-Roman pieces such as chairs, stools, couches and tables, and details such as the lion monopodium, lion foot, griffin and lyre, were all reproduced. Egyptian ornament included sphinx heads, winged lion supports and the lotus leaf (155). Dark, striped and glossy woods—mahogany,

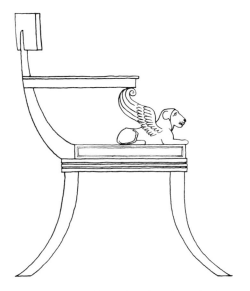

156 Grecian chair (from T. Hope 1807)

Many chairs were based on the ancient Greek 'klismos' (156), readily copied from vase paintings, which had rear legs and back forming a bold curve, balanced by forward curving ('sabre') front legs. The cresting was a wide board at shoulder height and usually extended beyond the uprights, which were joined by the arms near the top. These sabre legs and cresting boards (which often rested on the uprights) were common features of other types of chairs. 'Parlour' chairs of mahogany or rosewood were frequently inlaid with brass, while 'fancy' chairs of beech were painted or japanned, some of them having turned framework to imitate bamboo. The bergère type of armchair was popular, the continuous back, sides and seat being of canework. Also frequently seen were stools of X-shape construction, or with animal legs. Hope's designs for chairs with classical detail led to much wild use by his successors of animal forms for legs and arms.

A prominent Regency piece was the sofa or couch, used for reclining, and for a time more fashionable than the settee. One kind, based directly on classical models, had a boldly curved headpiece with a short arm rest, and a low, scrolled end, with legs that were either outward curved, lion-shaped, or turned in the form of a top. Another kind had two identical curved end-pieces joined by a padded back (157). The ottoman was a long, low seat without back or arms; a circular form was used for a room with a bow window or circular end.

Dining tables were still made in sets, often with pillar and claw supports, and were bolted together as required (162); but to avoid the bother of fitting these separate tables to each other, various kinds of extending tables became fashionable, some using a patent lazy-tongs method. Circular tables (163) were also found, on a pedestal base or pillar and claw. The Pembroke table (164) continued in wide use and often served as a tea table, but developing from it appeared the sofa table (158, 165) which had a

amboyna, calamander, zebrawood and above all rosewood—were much used, set off by bright brass mounts and given a brilliant finish by French polish, introduced about 1815. Rosewood was in great vogue not only for its suitable colour, but also because direct trade had been opened during the war with Brazil, its source of supply. Brass, in the form of inlay, galleries, colonnettes, beading, trellis-work, lion mask handles, feet and castors, was a characteristic decoration, being both cheaper and more durable than marquetry and carving (158, 159, 160). Reeding was also very popular as it accentuated straight structural lines (167). Much of the furniture was now lower in height so as to leave 'an ample space on the wall above for the placing of pictures' (Smith, 1808). For a time interior decoration became simpler; walls were painted plain colours or papered in bold patterns; upholstery and draperies were often striped. A certain amount of Gothic and Chinese furniture was also made. A Chinese revival, incorporating the usual oriental motives, and particularly making use of imitation bamboo on chairs and tables, usually in japanned beechwood, owed much to the Chinese interior given to Brighton Pavilion when it was rebuilt after 1815. It was altogether a period of such rapid change that T. Martin (*The Circle of the Mechanical Arts*, 1820) suggested that furniture designs, 'like female fashions, should be published monthly'.

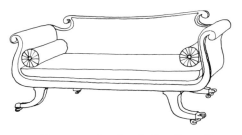

157 Regency painted and gilt sofa, c. 1810

158 Regency sofa table of rosewood inlaid with brass, *c.* 1820–5

159 Mahogany games and work-table, *c.* 1820–5. Rosewood footstool

160 Rosewood hanging bookshelves, *c.* 1810

161 Canterbury or music stand, *c.* 1810

162 Regency dining table

163 Regency round top table

164 Regency Pembroke table

166 Circular table (from T. Hope 1807)

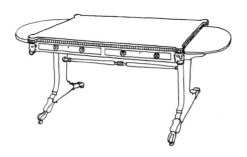

165 Sofa table (from Sheraton's *Encyclopaedia* 1804)

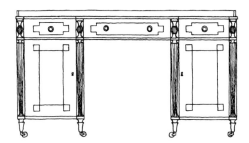

167 Regency mahogany sideboard

examples were made at first (167), they tended to become massive pieces of furniture. Later pedestals tapered slightly to floor level, above them were knife-boxes of the same tapered shape, and the central shelf had an ornamental back-piece. Sometimes side tables without pedestals were used, with a brass gallery. Under them stood a wine-cooler, commonly of sarcophagus shape.

Chests of drawers did not show any great change in structure, but in addition to the deep frieze above the top drawer, new features included lion-mask handles and reeded columns at the corners.

Soon after 1800 there was a great demand for the circular convex mirror (168), with a hollow moulding in the gilt frame usually filled with a row of gilt balls, a reeded outer edge, and an ebonised fillet next to the glass. More ambitious examples were surmounted by a carved eagle or acanthus leaves or honeysuckle, and had candle branches. Large chimney-glasses and pier glasses were placed in wealthier houses to reflect from room to room, and to catch, at night, the light of the great cut-glass chandeliers.

total length, with its end flaps raised on fly brackets, of some five or six feet. Its supports were either a pedestal on a small platform with splayed feet, or two end supports joined by a stretcher. This handy piece was chiefly for ladies' use, for drawing, reading or writing. The pedestal library table was now furnished with lion feet, Egyptian figures and other decorative details of the time. Round 'classical' tables had three or four lion monopodia or a single pedestal base (166). Various kinds of small portable tables were placed about the living rooms—nests of four ('quartetto') of different sizes (134), ladies' work tables with pouches for needlework, and combined reading, writing and games tables (159).

In addition to the traditional type of large bookcases, there were now a number of smaller ones which could be used in the living rooms and boudoir as well as the library (160). The rectangular dwarf bookcase, with doors which were either glazed or fitted with brass wire trellis, sometimes had an additional cabinet for curiosities. Revolving circular bookcases were a novelty, one kind being patented in 1808, the shelves turning around a central shaft. For ladies, there were tiny open shelves, sometimes with brass trellis sides, to move 'books for present reading' easily about the house. The chiffonier—the name previously for a small case of drawers on legs—was an open, low cupboard with shelves for books.

Lightness, however, was not a feature of Regency sideboards, for fashion swung back to the sideboard table and flanking cupboards of the Adam type, and although some neat combined

168 Regency mirror (from Smith 1808)

The Windsor Chair

A BRIEF reference can be made here to one of the most famous of English 'country' pieces, the 'stick-back' or Windsor chair, which has remained popular for some three centuries. The name 'Windsor' can be traced back to at least 1724, but its origin is a mystery, for the chair has no known connection with the royal town. Various native woods were used in its manufacture, but it commonly had an elm seat, beech spindles and legs, and a yew or ash frame. The early 'comb-back'(169) was gradually superseded after 1750 by the hoop-back(170). Both kinds often had a central splat imitating the decorative features of fashionable chairs. Other features frequently found were the curved stretcher, and front legs of cabriole form (148). Late Georgian types included a wheel or Prince of Wales's feathers in the back.

170 Windsor hoop-back chair, late eighteenth century

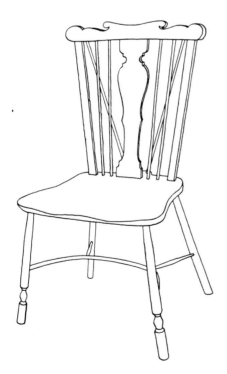

169 Comb-back Windsor chair, mid-eighteenth century

These cheap and light chairs were widely used in farmhouses, cottages, inns and tea-gardens (outdoor varieties were painted, usually in green), but they were also found in larger houses, some being fitted with book-rest arms for reading and writing.

Windsor chair-making was a widespread rural craft, but it has long been particularly associated with the High Wycombe area of Buckinghamshire. In the beechwoods around the town 'bodgers' turned the legs and spindles on their lathes, and benchmen made the seats, bows and splats. It was not until about 1850 that this woodland craft became a factory industry centred in High Wycombe, and even then some of the finest of all handmade Windsors were produced by an independent local craftsman, H. E. Goodchild (1885–1950), in his workshop at Naphill.

The Victorian Period

(1830–1901)

—————◇—————

General

THE beginning of Victoria's reign (1837–1901) coincided closely with the advent (1830) of the railway system, which quickened still more the pace of industrialisation and brought in the true Industrial Revolution. From the time of the Great Exhibition (1851) to the end of the reign Britain was the 'workshop of the world'. The rapid spread of mechanisation and of the factory system, coupled with the unprecedented rise in population (owing largely to advances in medical science and public health), led to the growth of great industrial cities, and thus to a greater demand for, and output of, furniture than ever before. Perhaps as much furniture was made in Victoria's reign as in all previous English history. About 1830 also, the long domination of classical taste finally ended, and was succeeded by experiments in historic styles, in which versions of the Gothic predominated. The effects of these economic and stylistic changes were in many ways deplorable. Though furniture itself was still made almost entirely by hand, the substitution of machinery for hand skills in other crafts had the result of filling Victorian homes with cheap and ill-designed articles which undermined both the whole basis of craftsmanship and the standard of taste of the purchasers, and furniture was inevitably affected by this debasement. Thus 1830 ushered in a revolution in furniture-making as

172 'Style of Francis I' carved oak cabinet: 1851 Exhibition

significant as those of the fifteenth and seventeenth centuries.

It would be a serious mistake, however, to dismiss all Victorian furniture as tasteless. The elaborate furniture shown at the Great Exhibition (171, 172, 180) and other exhibitions of the time was not, contrary to general belief, typical of the period, for its object, as was quickly pointed out, was 'startling novelties or meretricious decoration' (R. Redgrave, R.A., 1857). Much furniture was still well made, with excellent materials. Architects and designers increasingly turned their attention to producing good and interesting furniture, and by the end of the century there was a remarkable revival of craftsmanship for which William Morris was chiefly responsible.

It is unfortunate that these developments must be set against the background of mass-produced furniture in debased versions of current styles, turned out by the numerous firms in all the large cities—for the dominance of both London and the court had now gone.

Early Victorian

(1830–1860)

The guiding feature of early Victorian furniture was its emphasis on comfort, very understandable

171 'Elizabethan' table and stool, early Victorian: 1851 Exhibition

at a time when a larger proportion of English people than ever before had homes and furniture of their own. Seat furniture was covered with well-padded upholstery, as cheap covering materials were now available, particularly worsteds from the Yorkshire power-loom factories, and Berlin wool-work, embroidery done in coloured wools on canvas from a large number of designs. It was also the custom to cover tables with draperies, hiding all except the bottom of the legs. For the first time, the upholstery on furniture was more important than its wooden framework, and an elegant structural form was no longer the main consideration. Other kinds of furniture followed the pattern set by upholstered pieces. The straight lines and rectangular forms of the Regency were replaced by rounded corners, curves, and oval or semicircular plans; projecting members were generally discarded; and separate parts were welded into a unity. Surfaces were left plain and brightly finished in French polish, for inlay, ormolu and coloured woods were out of fashion, and even handles were of wood and not of metal.

By 1835 two revivals, the Louis XIV and the Elizabethan, were firmly established, though 'Grecian' and Gothic (173) furniture continued to be made. The Louis XIV style (which included much of the Louis XV) came from France after the Bourbon restoration and led to the use of baroque and rococo scrollwork on drawing-room and bedroom furniture (174). The Elizabethan revival, which its supporters distinguished from the Gothic, though it is often impossible to separate them, combined 'the Gothic with the Roman or Italian manner' (J. C. Loudon, 1833). It owed much to Henry Shaw's *Specimens of Ancient Furniture* (1836) and similar books, and to the strongly-held belief that it was a vigorous, independent English style full of romantic associations. It largely took the form of strapwork carving on tables (171), mirrors and sideboards. Despite much criticism both these revivals had a long vogue. The pattern books, such as Henry

173 'Gothic' sideboard, early Victorian
(from J. C. Loudon 1833)

174 Pier table 'Louis XIV style' (from
J. C. Loudon 1833)

Whitaker's *Treasury of Designs* (1847) tried hard to capture these styles, sometimes with fair success, sometimes with much eclectic confusion. There was also a 'Francis I' style which used early Renaissance decoration (172).

There were two original developments in chair design in this period, the balloon-back and prie-dieu. The balloon-back evolved from the modification of both the standard form of classical dining-room and parlour chair as it was made in 1830, with broad cresting rail overrunning the uprights, carved horizontal splat and straight legs (177), and the Louis XIV drawing-room chair with scrolls on rail and splat. By 1835 the rail on all types had been rounded, and between 1835-50 both rail and uprights formed a continuous curve narrowed at the waist by the splat. The balloon-back was popular until well after 1860, some versions having (from 1850) cabriole legs (178). The prie-dieu had a tall, fully-upholstered back, and low seat and short legs, both the latter and the uprights being often twist-turned (179). It was apparently based on the Charles II cane chair, but in the prevailing confusion of stylistic dating it was considered to be a typical Tudor design, and even versions with carved cresting were called 'Elizabethan' chairs. The prie-dieu was a good example of the over-riding consideration of comfort as also were 'lounging' (easy) and library chairs with their round, padded backs, and the larger types of seating furniture. The sofa, for instance, became padded all over, the back and arms forming a continuous whole, and the only exposed woodwork was that of the short legs. The ottoman was usually a covered box with a central back which gave seats on two or all four sides.

175

175 Early Victorian rosewood what-not with drawer in topmost tier

176 Papier-mâché tea-poy in which the caddies of green and black tea were kept locked, *c.* 1835

176

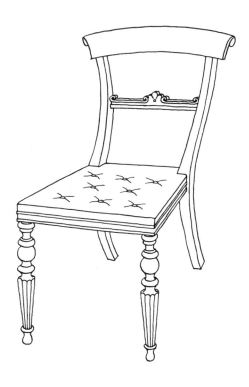

177 'Grecian' chair, early Victorian
(from J. C. Loudon 1833)

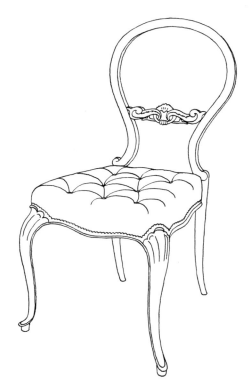

178 Balloon-back chair, c. 1850

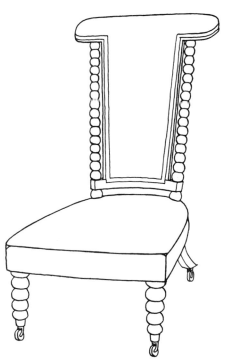

179 Prie-dieu chair, early Victorian

180 'The day dreamer' papier-mâché chair:
1851 Exhibition

Tables showed little change from Regency kinds, except that supports on circular tables tended to become rather heavy curves. Sideboards, on the other hand, showed distinct changes and illustrated the fashion for rounding off corners. In 1830 they were still rectangular and of pedestal form; by 1840 mirrors were added to the back, usually a large one in the centre and two smaller flanking ones; the central mirror was then raised higher than the others, and all three had semicircular crests. The pedestals were rounded off, giving the sideboard a semicircular plan as well as a semicircular elevation. Similarly the chiffonier, now used in dining-rooms which were too small for a large sideboard, acquired a mirror-back, glass or wooden doors, and round, open shelves at each side. A new piece, already known but now in regular use for the first time, was the what-not, a stand in the form of open shelves with turned columns at the corners (175).

Experiments were made during this period, especially at the Great Exhibition, where they were widely advertised, to use a variety of materials, e.g. metals and patent substances, instead of wood for furniture. Like the ornate furniture at the Exhibition, however, many of these substitutes had only limited application. Some iron furniture was used for halls and gardens, but attempts to make indoor furniture of this kind proved unsuccessful. Brass beds, on the other hand, became popular in the late 1840's. Papier-mâché furniture was also made (176, 180), but as most of it came from one firm, Jennens and Bettridge, who normally produced trays and boxes, it formed only a minute part of the furniture of the time. The only other wood substitute to affect furniture design was Italian marble, which was widely used for washstand tops in bedrooms.

Late Victorian
(1860–1901)

While after 1860 the great mass of furniture remained deplorably uninspired (it was in this period that the trade gave 'veneer' its secondary meaning of a superficially attractive exterior masking something essentially shoddy), there were nevertheless two important developments in furniture design. One sprang from William Morris (1834–96), whose life work restored much of the regard for good craftsmanship and culminated in the Arts and Crafts Movement at the end of the century; the other proceeded from

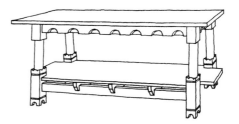

181 Table designed by Philip Webb, *c.* 1870

architects and artists who pursued their own styles with honesty and understanding.

Morris was horrified at the dismal aesthetic standards of his day, and saw that just as the agricultural revolution had wiped out the independent English peasant, so the industrial revolution threatened to destroy the craftsman. In 1861 he founded a firm, Morris & Co. (which

182 Morris & Co. chair adapted from a traditional Sussex type, *c.* 1865

lasted until 1940), to produce beautiful, hand-made objects for the home, and spent the rest of his life, as artist, craftsman, writer and socialist, preaching that art was 'the expression by man of his pleasure in labour'. Though his products were normally too expensive for most people, and he was not himself particularly interested in furniture, his firm yet contrived to turn out some fine

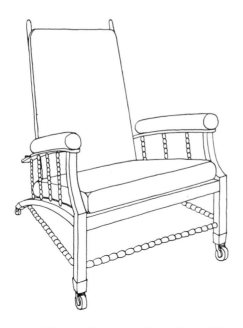

183 Morris & Co. adjustable chair, *c.* 1866

furniture, much of it at a low price. The architect, Philip Webb (1831–1915), designed for him tables in unstained oak which deliberately left the joints exposed to prove their honest workmanship (181). After 1865 a popular cheap rush-bottomed chair, based on an old country type seen by Morris in Sussex, was made in large quantities (182). Equally popular was a drawing-room easy chair (183) with adjustable back (still known in America as the 'Morris chair' owing to its great success there). The artist, Ford Madox Brown (1821–93) also designed cheap bedroom furniture for the firm. Morris refused to compromise with machinery ('production by machinery is altogether an evil') and thus never considered that designing simple, effective objects for quick and cheap production by machines might be a worth-while aim. He was also unable to free himself from the belief in the supremacy of mediaeval craft, of which, in his enthusiasm, he took an exaggerated view. What might he have accomplished had he cleared his mind of these two prejudices?

Meanwhile, in the late 1860's, a new version of the Gothic was developed which more than any other may be ranked as the most distinguishable late Victorian style. It was initiated by Bruce Talbert (1838–81) (186) and C. L. Eastlake (1836–1906), and popularised by the latter's book, *Hints on Household Taste* (1868). Case furniture, in

contrast to the former curves and plain surfaces, now emphasised straight lines, panelled construction and varied surface colour, not only with staining and painting, but also with materials like leather, metals and tiles. The architect, T. E. Collcutt (1840–1924) added a lively touch to the style with delicate painted panels and small shelves for knick-knacks. Upholstered furniture tended to have more of its framework visible. Unfortunately, in the hands of the trade Collcutt's designs led to a proliferation of what-nots, corner cupboards and overmantels, overloaded with shelves and pigeon-holes and tiny, turned baluster railings.

Quite separate from this was the Anglo-Japanese style which emerged in the 1870's and 1880's, following the opening-up of Japan and exhibitions of Japanese crafts. E. W. Godwin (1833–86), another architect, ingeniously translated this Japanese style into light and graceful furniture with slender supports and skilled balance of space and solid (184), but once again the indiscriminate spread of the style, particularly its imitation bamboo legs and fretwork panels, brought it into disrepute.

At the end of Victoria's reign furniture design was dominated by the Arts and Crafts Movement, the name given to numerous societies which arose after 1880 to make and exhibit articles of good craftsmanship. This was one of the most potent results of Morris's work. It would be wrong, however, to assume that the movement concentrated on making austere oak furniture of the kind designed by Webb for Morris in the 1860's, great though its influence undoubtedly was (187), for there was an equally strong move towards more decorative furniture, both in the eighteenth

184 E. W. Godwin ebonised cabinet in the Japanese style, 1877

185

Late Victorian

185 Sideboard, painted by E. Burne-Jones, founder member of Morris & Co., 1860

186 Walnut cabinet by Bruce Talbert

187 Oak table, *c.* 1880

188 Writing-desk designed by C. F. A. Voysey 1896

187

186

188

189 Ernest Gimson ash chair stained black, *c.* 1910

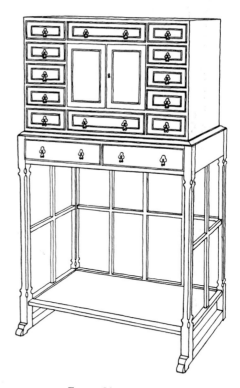

190 Ernest Gimson cabinet, 1910

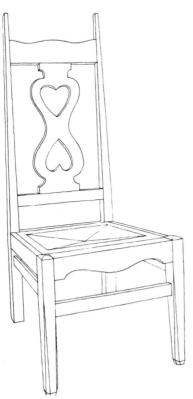

191 C. F. A. Voysey chair, 1896

192 Mackintosh painted chair, *c.* 1900

193 Oak dresser designed and made by Sidney Barnsley and shown at the 1899 exhibition of the Arts and Crafts Exhibition Society

century tradition, and in the direction of incorporating into furniture the work (in e.g. leather, glass and metal) of other craftsmen.

The greatest artist-craftsman of this movement was Ernest Gimson (1864–1920) who abandoned his career as an architect to go to the Cotswolds where, with the two brothers, Sidney and Ernest Barnsley (193), he established a workshop and designed some outstanding furniture. He was very responsive to English tradition in both his simpler pieces (189) and in his cabinets (190) and the like, with their austere and elegant outlines and fine surface decoration. Other important figures were the architects C. F. A. Voysey (1857–1941), whose light and simple interiors were màtched by his bold (if sometimes eccentric) furniture (188, 191), and C. R. Mackintosh (1868–1928) (192).

Modern

194 Table in Australian black-
bean inlaid holly and sycamore
by Edward Barnsley

195 Cabinet of drawers in walnut
with serpentine front by Edward
Barnsley

196 Walnut china cabinet by
Edward Barnsley, 1959

194

196

195

The Twentieth Century

PROGRESS towards good design has been sadly hampered in the present century by the impact of machine-made furniture, which was already clearly heralded before 1900. For mass-produced furniture has clung obstinately to imitating traditional forms, often debased, and has tried to make by machine what should only properly be made by hand. Thus in the post-war building boom of the twenties, when rapid production was the sole aim, the furniture in mock-Tudor, Jacobean and other styles, poor in design, materials and construction, must rank among the worst ever made here. It has been largely left to foreigners to lead the 'modern movement', the general name for the whole re-appraisal of design in relation to production by machine and the use of modern materials. The 'furniture-architects' of Germany and Scandinavia have shown that it was not machines in themselves which made inferior furniture, but the inability of designers to use machines properly. Scandinavian machine-made furniture in particular, with its clean lines and imaginative use of new materials like plywood and bentwood, has had a great influence (though it should be mentioned that bentwood furniture

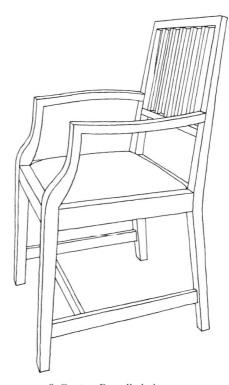

198 Gordon Russell chair, 1920–30

was made abroad by Michael Thonet as early as the 1830's).

England, however, has produced two outstandingly successful figures in the field of design for both machine- and hand-made furniture. Sir Ambrose Heal (1872–1959) was a product of the Arts and Crafts Movement. Trained as a cabinet-maker, he won a silver medal at the Paris Exhibition of 1900 for a bedroom suite, and after taking over the family business in London, turned to the production of good, progressive furniture, of strong but simple and beautiful lines (197). Sir Gordon Russell (b. 1892) set up business at Broadway after the First World War, and, beginning with furniture in the Gimson tradition, later also developed factory production of well-designed, finely-made furniture (198). A particularly high standard was achieved with radio cabinets, the design of which matched the precision of their contents as successfully as the cases of late Stuart clocks matched the mechanism

197 Ambrose Heal bedroom cupboard

199 Edward Barnsley side table

of their movements. Russell was also largely responsible for the design of 'utility' furniture during the Second World War, when there was a great timber shortage. The result was to provide the public with a complete range of furniture of good construction, simple and attractive lines, at a reasonable price.

The unquestioned leader of the group of craftsmen who have continued the Gimson tradition of fine hand craftsmanship is Edward Barnsley (b. 1900), the son of Sidney Barnsley, whose workshop at Petersfield has produced furniture worthy to rank with the finest of the past (194, 195, 196, 199). It is inspired by the best traditions in English design but has carried them forward with full appreciation of new methods and materials, and the needs of a new age.

Index

Figures in **bold** type refer to illustration numbers